inside
soccer

inside
soccer
for beginners

klaus ruege

Contemporary Books, Inc.
Chicago

contents

acknowledgments

The author would like to thank the many kind people who helped make this book possible, including Joyce Black, administrative assistant, for her preparation of the manuscript; the members of the Northbrook Kickers soccer team, for helping to illustrate the book; Dr. Helmut Kaser of FIFA for permission to reprint the Laws of the Game; and the following North American Soccer League officials: Brad Sham and Jim Walker of the Chicago Sting, Paul Ridings of the Dallas Tornado, John Chaffetz of the Los Angeles Aztecs, Ralph Wright of the Miami Toros, Steve Weaver of the St. Louis Stars, Tom Mertens of the San Jose Earthquakes, Jim Trecker of the New York Cosmos, and Richard Dorfman of the Washington Diplomats.

The author would also like to express his gratitude to the following organizations for supplying the photographs that illustrate the book:

Chicago Sting, photos 5, 9, 10, 11, 21, 22, 25, 26, 32, 38, 39, 40, 41, 42, 44, 48, 61, 64
Dallas Tornado, photos 8, 13, 33
Los Angeles Aztecs, photos 15, 58
Miami Toros, photos 14, 43, 55, 57
New York Cosmos, photo 63
St. Louis Stars, photos 7, 29, 31, 49, 59
San Jose Earthquakes, photos 30, 35, 60
Washington Diplomats, photos 6, 56

introduction

"Why don't you Americans play soccer?"

Time and time again this question used to be thrown at me by my foreign friends and business associates during my overseas trips. I never had a good answer. Like others deeply involved in American soccer, I found the question both irritating and perplexing. While the rest of the world had accepted soccer upon introduction, the United States had seemingly regarded it with nearly total indifference, even though organized soccer had been played on the East Coast as early as the 1860s.

On my overseas trips today, the question I'm asked is not "Why don't Americans play?" but "Why are they playing it on such a vast scale?" It seems that all sports fans abroad have heard about the phenomenal growth of U.S. soccer, which has surprised even the most optimistic of soccer boosters.

I always tell them that the big breakthrough for American soccer came in 1966 when the World Cup final was shown on American television. The enthusiastic reception of millions of American viewers prompted over a score of prominent American business tycoons to form not one but two professional soccer leagues. One of them, the North American Soccer League, is still with us, thriving and expanding in cities throughout the country. It is the NASL to whom most credit must be

PHOTO 1. The author with one of his youth teams.

given for soccer's emergence as a major sport in the U.S. The exposure it gave to the general public—the publicity it received in the press, on radio, and especially on television—awakened school and college administrators to the many advantages offered by the game.

After a hundred years American educators began to recognize the unmatchable qualities of soccer. What other sport permitted all sizes to participate, was a superb body conditioner, was relatively injury-free, and required so little equipment that it was a low-cost item on any school budget? In addition to all this, the educators soon discovered—as did other Americans—that soccer is a nonstop action sport that is at once simple to understand, exciting to play, and breathtaking to watch.

I hope the reader of this book will discover for himself how exciting soccer is by joining a team and getting into the action. I think you'll soon see why soccer is the number-one sport in the world.

PHOTO 2. To prove that size is unimportant in soccer, look at player number 7, seen here scoring a goal. This diminutive youngster, half the size of most of his opponents, was his team's top scorer in the 1975 season.

PHOTO 3. The author looks on as members of his visiting youth team train with the famous Schalke 04 team of Germany.

PHOTO 4. A good appearance helps to build confidence and team spirit. Don't show up for games in dirty or torn uniforms.

chapter 1
EQUIPMENT

The trend in modern soccer is to dress as lightly as possible: lightweight shoes, jerseys, and shorts, and thin shinpads. The reason for this, of course, is to eliminate any weight that will slow down the player in a sport where speed is of such importance.

As I mentioned in the introduction, soccer equipment is inexpensive. However, spending a little extra on soccer shoes is always a good investment. Not that there is anything wrong with the all-purpose baseball-football-soccer shoe offered by Sears, Montgomery Ward, and Penney's, but the extra refinements featured in the better shoe will benefit the more experienced player.

The toecap, for instance, is quite often harder and less flexible on the cheaper shoe than that on an Adidas, Puma, Gola, or other top-quality shoe. Padded backs, padded tongues, and padded achilles tendon supports are also items that cannot be expected on a cheaper shoe; nor will you find detachable studs (cleats) or leather uppers. But despite all the extras that come with the $20-to-$30 shoes, there is a lot to be said for a beginner starting off his soccer career with an $8-to-$10 all-purpose shoe.

The main thing is to make certain your shoe fits snugly and that the studs do not project more than ¾ inch from the sole—anything bigger is considered dangerous under the laws of the game.

If you can afford it, buy shoes with interchangeable studs. Use the rubber studs for hard ground and either leather or nylon studs for the wet and muddy fields.

Once you have purchased your shoes, don't forget to clean them after each game so that they stay free of mud. A wet rag will do fine; a little saddle soap even better. Try using some leather softener occasionally to help keep the shoe soft and pliable. Your shoes can last for many years with a little care.

Soccer jerseys (shirts) and shorts are usually provided by the team, so there is no need for beginning players to worry about their cost. The majority of jerseys and shorts today are made of nylon, rayon, dureen, and cotton mixtures. Most soccer leagues now insist upon numbers on the back of the shirt and some are experimenting with numbers on both the front and the back for easier identification.

Shorts seem to be getting shorter and shorter. There was a time when shorts reached down to the knees, but not anymore. Today they come down only as far as the upper thighs—which, as you can imagine, provides little comfort on cold days. Nevertheless, they are definitely more utilitarian than the old baggy shorts of the pre-1950 days, as they are cut with extra width around the legs for extra freedom of movement.

Because he is permitted to use his hands, the goalkeeper has to wear a jersey of a different color from that of his team. In addition, his jersey must contrast with the uniforms of his opponents, so most goalkeepers have jerseys in at least two colors. The jersey is always of one solid color.

As with the rest of the team, the goalkeeper should if possible wear a heavy jersey in colder weather and a lighter one on warmer days. Quite often on extremely cold days a goalkeeper will wear a pair of sweatpants or a warm-up suit.

Most goalkeepers today, pros and amateurs alike, wear gloves, especially on wet and cold days. The modern glove has small rubber dots on its cotton or wool surface that do much to help the goalkeeper control the wet slippery ball. This type of glove can cost from $8 to $15.

Shinguards are splendid protection against cuts and bruises but appear to be out of fashion with many college and professional players. I recommend them for everyone, despite the trend away from them. The newer ones are very thin and lightweight and should not slow you down once you get used to them. For an outlay of three to four dollars, shinpads could well be the best investment of all.

Soccer balls are another item your team will provide, but it is always a good idea to have a ball of your own to practice with. In recent years the laws relating to soccer balls have been relaxed to the point where just about any type of material can be used for the outer covering. The laws of the game still state that ". . . the outer casing shall be of leather or any other approved materials . . ."—but more and more we are seeing the synthetic balls taking over from the leather balls.

The best soccer balls will have 32 panels, either leather or synthetic, and will be waterproofed with a plastic coating. Many will have a built-in balance, which has practically eliminated the swerving or dropping of hard-hit balls. The Danish company Select offers an excellent balanced ball—as do Adidas and Mitre.

For juvenile soccer, the official size #5 ball can be substituted with a #4, which is smaller and much easier for youngsters to maneuver.

As with your shoes, care must be taken to clean and polish your ball. Whenever it is not being used for long periods of time make sure you deflate it or else it will stretch.

Before we leave equipment, a few words about eyeglasses. There is no rule against their use in soccer, but it obviously can be dangerous to wear glasses in a game. I advise all my players wearing them to turn their heads whenever an opponent kicks at a nearby ball. This may not be good soccer coaching but it is, I believe, a most sensible preventive act for anyone who wants to enjoy playing the game without suffering an injury to the eye. If you decide you want to take up soccer seriously then you might want to consider contact lenses.

PHOTO 5. Expect the unexpected: the Chicago Sting's Gordon Hill (10), the star of the 1975 NASL season, prepares to use a scissors kick to kick the ball over his head. (Photo—Bill Smith)

chapter 2
THE GAME OF SOCCER

The element of surprise pervades the game of soccer from the moment the ball is kicked off until the final whistle. Its speed, fluidity, and continuous movement from one goal to the other invite the unexpected, and the constant changing of possession from team to team gives little opportunity for set plays.

This is one sport that cannot be orchestrated with pre-game planning. Instead, the swirling flow of the game demands on-the-spot creativity and individual decision-making by the player in control of the ball. To dribble to the left, to run to the right, to pass to a teammate 40 yards away, to shoot; it's all up to him, and whatever he decides he must do it quickly. There is not time to consider locker-room strategy or a numbered play.

But this absence of set plays does not mean tactics or team formations are absent in soccer. Far from it. In recent years the trend has been for the game to become over-organized; team positions have changed and the accent on defensive play is, unfortunately, all too evident, particularly on the professional level.

TEAM POSITIONS

For the first eighty years of organized soccer the accepted lineup at the beginning of a game corresponded to that shown in Diagram A. Today, although some people still talk about center halfs, halfbacks, inside forwards, and center forwards, most of these names have been discarded. As Diagram B indicates, the team is now divided into three sections: the defense, the mid-field, and the attack. It is a much simpler method of identifying players and is also a truer picture of what duties each player has.

The Goalkeeper

His name is still the same but even this un-soccer-like specialist's role has changed over the years. The only man on the team who can touch the ball with his hands, and

DIAGRAM A

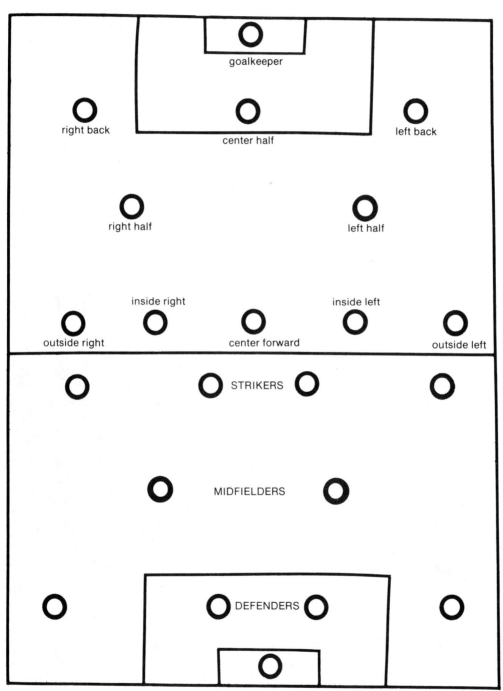

goalkeeper

right back

center half

left back

right half

left half

inside right

inside left

outside right

center forward

outside left

STRIKERS

MIDFIELDERS

DEFENDERS

DIAGRAM B

more of a circus acrobat than a soccer player, the goalie can no longer be content with simply stopping the ball from entering the net. Every time he possesses the ball he must think of attack. Modern soccer demands that his goal kicks, clearances, and throwing must be thoughtful and constructive. (See chapter Five for a fuller description of goalkeepers.)

The Defenders

The four defenders—right back, right center back, left center back, and left back—form the heart of the defense. Sometimes in junior soccer, and very often in adult soccer, they are given a boost by the addition of a "sweeper," a player who stays back behind the four to "sweep up" anyone who breaks through.

All of the defenders, either four of five, have basic responsibilities no matter which defensive position they are assigned. All must try to gain possession of the ball from their opponents and, if this is not possible, to delay, impede, and in general make things so uncomfortable for their opponents that mistakes will be committed.

To protect their own goal and goalkeeper is, of course, the defenders' main task. To accomplish this they must dominate their own penalty area with numerical superiority, tight guarding (marking), strong tackling, accurate clearances of loose balls (with the feet or head), and absolute confidence in heading away the high balls that come across or through the penalty area.

In most defensive systems the right back guards the opposing left striker (outside left); the center backs handle the center of the defense and stay close to the central strikers; and the left back has the right striker (outside right) as his responsibility.

PHOTO 6. The Goalkeeper: the only man permitted to play the ball with the hands.

PHOTO 7. Heading away the high ball. Defender Pat McBride of the St. Louis Stars jumps high to clear his line.

In chapter eight we will take a closer look at how the defense operates in the framework of the man-to-man and zonal systems. We will also see how modern soccer has given defenders the opportunity to participate in offensive play as well.

The Midfieldmen

I can't think of one great team of the last 20 years that did not have a powerful midfield line, and as far as I'm concerned the midfield is the most important part of a soccer team.

Assigned the task of linking up the defensive unit with the team's offense, the midfieldmen are both defenders and attackers. Often called the engine room of the team, the midfielders do more running

than anyone else on the team and thus have to be in perfect physical condition. In modern soccer the midfielders (or halfbacks, as they used to be called) have become more important than ever. The old saying, "whoever controls the midfield controls the game," still rings true, particularly now that midfieldmen are expected to go up and score much more than in the past.

The dual role of the midfielder means that he must be a strong tackler while helping out his defensive colleagues and a nimble imaginative artist with the ball when moving upfield. Normally he keeps an eye on the opposing midfieldmen when they get the ball, but he must also be ready to drop back and relieve any of the defenders when they are hard pressed or outnumbered. In attack he helps provide depth by moving up behind his strikers so that his strikers can pass back to him to form triangular passing movements. Quite often a midfielder will engage in a quick

PHOTO 8. One of the top NASL stars since its inception, midfielder Ilija Mitic drops back to help his defense. (Photo—Jim Work)

give-and-go with a striker around the penalty area, enabling the striker to get into a scoring position. At other times it will be the midfielder who accepts a return pass from the striker and shoots for goal.

But above all, the midfieldmen's main job is to take command of the area between the two penalty areas and attempt to dictate the flow and pace of the game.

The Strikers

For many years now, superior coaches have been saying that there are no longer attackers or defenders, that it is the possession or nonpossession of the ball that dictates whether you are defending or attacking. Nevertheless, it is usually members of the offensive line who still put the ball into the back of the net.

Whether it is a three-, four-, or five-man attacking line, it is the strikers who see most action around the opponent's penalty area. In the usual four-man line, the outside attackers are either called wingers or outside strikers; the two men in the center of the action are called central strikers.

The wingers generally are the carriers of the team, transporting the ball at top speed down the flanks before passing it into the center for the central strikers or midfieldmen to hammer into the net. Ball control, speed, clever dribbling, and accurate passing ability are essential requirements for a good winger.

The central strikers are usually selected for their position because of their shooting prowess and heading ability. In the majority of cases the strikers are big men (big for soccer, that is), over six feet tall and powerful enough to withstand the constant buffeting and body jarring that take place in the closely guarded penalty area. In the earlier days of soccer the hallmark of a top central striker (or center forward, as he was called) was his sheer size and strength. Today, however, he must also be agile,

quick off the mark, and skillful at eluding the many defenders patrolling the penalty area.

Because he is often facing his own goal when he receives a pass, a striker must be adept at turning with the ball in tight situations. Similarly, his ball control has to be first-rate, as does his skill at screening the ball from opponents. All in all, the central striker has the toughest job in soccer. He is so closely guarded that he may not touch the ball more than twenty times during a game, but when he does break through it is the most exciting moment in the game.

THE RULES

Thanks to the foresight of its founders, soccer is a simple game to understand. The rules are easy to follow, and fifteen minutes of viewing a game should be sufficient for the average sports fan to know what is going on. Mastering the intricate skills of soccer is another story, of course, which we will go into later.

PHOTO 9. Facing his own goal, striker Russell Allen of the Chicago Sting is closely guarded by two San Jose defenders as he brings the ball down with his chest. (Photo—Bill Smith)

The rules (see Appendix for the complete Laws of the Game), seventeen in all, are all aimed at keeping the game moving, with as few stoppages as possible. The ultimate aim is to score goals (never called points), and if possible, more goals than your opponents. As in football, equal scores at the end of the game result in a tie game (also called a draw in soccer).

Although soccer is basically a kicking game, the chest and head are also used in propelling the ball. In fact, any part of the body can be employed excepting the hands and the arms. Goalkeepers are the only ones permitted to touch the ball with the hands and arms.

There are eleven players on each team and the prescribed time period is 90 minutes, divided into two halves of 45 minutes each. In junior soccer this is often reduced to 60 minutes of play (two 30-minute halves or four 15-minute quarters). The goal posts are eight yards wide and eight feet high. All fields must be greater in length than in width but can vary from 100 to 130 yards in length and from 50 to 100 yards in width. Diagram C is a model of the average full-size soccer field, the size used for international games.

The infringements in soccer are divided in two: major fouls, which are penalized by the awarding of direct free kicks; and lesser violations, which are penalized by the awarding of indirect free kicks. In direct free kick situations, goals can be scored directly from the kick, but when an indirect free kick is given, a goal can be scored only if a second person from either team has touched the ball after the kick has been taken.

Briefly, the major fouls are:

1. Kicking or attempting to kick an opponent.

2. Tripping or trying to trip an opponent.

3. Charging an opponent in a violent or dangerous manner.

4. Charging an opponent from behind unless the latter is obstructing.

5. Jumping at an opponent.

6. Striking or attempting to strike an opponent.

7. Holding an opponent.

8. Pushing an opponent.

9. Handling the ball (other than the goalkeeper within his own penalty area).

The minor fouls are:

1. Playing in a manner considered by the referee to be dangerous.

2. Shoulder charging when the ball is not within playing distance.

3. Intentionally obstructing an opponent when not playing the ball.

4. Charging the goalie, except when he is holding the ball, is obstructing an opponent, or when he is outside his goal area.

5. Carrying the ball (when playing as a goalkeeper) more than four steps without releasing it.

6. Offside.

Any time a direct free kick is given against the defending team in its own penalty area, it results in a penalty kick. The ball is placed on the penalty spot, 12 yards from the goal, and only the goalkeeper is permitted to stop the shot. All other players on both teams (other than the player taking the penalty) must be out of the penalty area. Since the goalie must stay on his line and cannot move until after the kick has been taken, it should be no surprise that the odds are with the kicker.

No summary of the rules of soccer would be complete without a special reference to the offside law. Although clearly written, the offside law causes more trouble, on and off the field, than anything else in soccer. The rule states that an offensive player must have two opponents between him and the defender's goal line when the ball is played toward him. It is not when the

DIAGRAM C

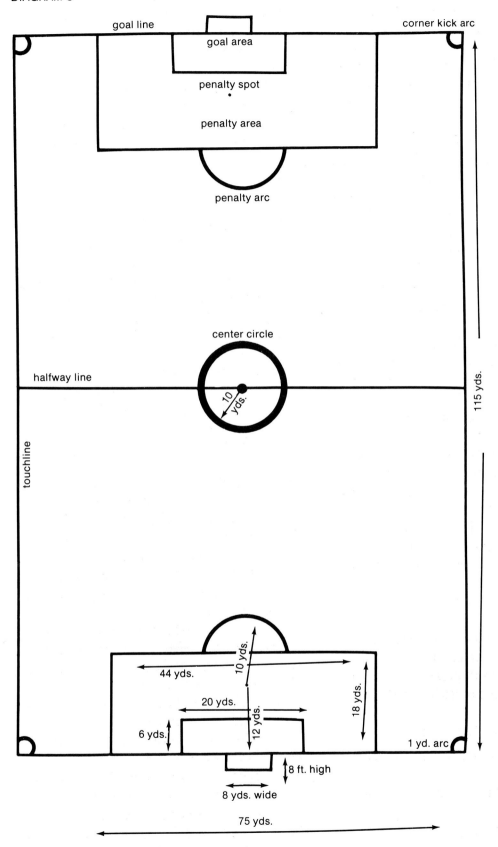

PHOTO 10. With the rest of the two teams looking on from outside the penalty area, Chicago Sting's Gordon Hill beats goalie Ken Cooper of the Dallas Tornado. (Photo—Don Garfinkel)

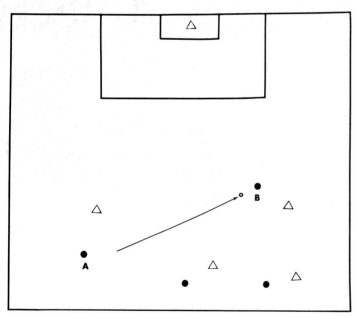

DIAGRAM D. OFFSIDE. B is offside, since there is only one opponent between him and the goal line when A passes the ball to him.

ponents when the ball is played toward him, and quite often a referee's judgment may differ from just about everyone else's on the field.

There are three exceptions to the general offside rule that allow you to be closer to your opponent's goal line than he:

1. When you are standing in your own half of the field.

2. When the ball comes to you after an opponent has touched it or played it.

3. When you receive the ball directly from a goal kick, corner kick, throw-in, or when it has been dropped by the referee.

THE REFEREE

The control of the game is completely in the hands of the one referee. He has the final word on everything that takes place on the field. He is assisted by two linesmen, whose primary task is simply deciding when the ball goes over the touchlines (sidelines) and

player gets the ball but when it is played toward him that counts. Unfortunately, it is difficult at times to determine where a player is standing in relation to his op-

goal lines, necessitating throw-ins, goal kicks, and corner kicks, and to assist the referee in spotting offside infringements. Quite often the referee will go over to the touchline to consult with a linesman on a particularly difficult call, but he is not required to accept the linesman's advice.

Because the referee is the all-powerful judge on the soccer field, it is only good sense for players not to be disrespectful or to argue with him. He has the power to eject players from the game for dissent and ungentlemanly conduct, so beware!

Cooperating with the referee is important for another reason, too. Soccer should be a game of constant movement, but a harassed referee is quite likely going to transform it into a frustrating series of shrill whistle blasts, endless stoppages, and stern lectures.

PHOTO 11. The referee gives the signal that indicates a goal has been scored. (Photo—Bill Smith)

PHOTO 12. The toe is pointed down for the instep kick.

chapter 3
THE ART OF KICKING

Although there are numerous ways of kicking a soccer ball, most newcomers to the sport tend to use one basic kick: a mighty lunge at the ball with the big toe, followed by a high swing of the leg like some ungainly Kung Fu novice. To overcome this tendency, beginners should always ask themselves before kicking, "What do I want to accomplish with this kick? A pass? A shot at goal? A clearance away from my own goal line? Do I want to keep the ball on the ground or do I want to lift it over an opponent's head? Can I reach it with my right foot or should I use my left? Is the ball coming to me on the ground or waist-high?" All these questions have to be answered in a split second, and it takes a great amount of practice and experience before the right decision comes naturally and quickly.

No matter what type of kick is used, the following fundamentals should be observed:

1. Keep your eye on the ball when kicking.
2. Position your nonkicking foot in the correct spot.
3. Strike the ball with the correct part of the foot.
4. Permit the kicking leg to follow through after striking the ball. And last but certainly not least,
5. Avoid kicking with the big toe.

Excepting for emergencies when nothing else can reach the ball, the toe is usually pointed down, as in the instep kick, which is probably the most important of all kicking styles.

THE INSTEP KICK

Photo 12 shows clearly the position of the toe at the time of contact. By pointing it down, a larger surface area of the foot is able to come into contact with the ball. This wraparound action gives power to the kick and is the reason why it is used for hard shots at goal, long passes, and, as we will see later, for volleys and half volleys.

PHOTO 13. A perfect example of the low instep kick by Bobby Moffat of the Dallas Tornado.

PHOTO 14. Ronnie Sharp of the Miami Toros follows through after a shot at goal. (Photo—John Pineda)

The Low Instep Kick

In photo 13 the nonkicking foot's position is a few inches behind the ball, the kicking leg is cocked for the back swing, the ankle is tensed, and the arms are held out for balance. In photo 14 the kick has been executed and we see the correct follow-through, a rhythmic swing that continues until it reaches near waist level. The harder the kick, the more likely it will be for the nonkicking foot to take a short hop to retain balance.

The Lofted Instep Kick

To use the instep to shoot or pass into the air, the nonkicking foot is placed farther behind the ball than for the low instep kick. The kicking foot aims for the lower half of the ball so that the foot can swing under the ball after it has been kicked. This swinging motion is helped by the body leaning backwards.

THE INSIDE-OF-THE-FOOT KICK

This is the safest and most accurate type of kick. As photo 16 shows, the whole inside of the foot hits the ball with the area between the base of the big toe and the anklebone the preferred contact point. The

PHOTO 15. Uri Banhoffer of the Los Angeles Aztecs gets set for a lofted instep kick.

kicking foot should be one or two inches off the ground, the toes should be pointed upwards, the ankle tensed, and the non-kicking foot alongside the ball at a right angle. Because of its limited back swing and shorter follow-through, the inside-of-the-foot kick (also called the push pass) is not as powerful as the instep kick and is normally used for short passes. It is, however, used nearly as much as the instep and must be mastered early in a player's career. When executed properly, it is the most attractive of all soccer motions. Two pros who use this kick with splendid accuracy are Al Trost of the St. Louis Stars and Esteban Aranguiz of the Miami Toros. Go and see them in action and try to emulate their actions.

PHOTO 16. The inside-of-the-foot kick.

THE OUTSIDE-OF-THE-FOOT KICK

A kick growing in popularity, the outside-of-the-foot kick can be used both for passing and (when mastered) quick devastating shots at goal when there is little time for the usual back swing.

The point of contact is shown in photo 17. Notice that the foot is turned slightly inward so that the outside of the instep strikes the ball. The leg swing is slight and moves across the ball instead of through it as in the instep kick. For best results, curl your toes down as you kick.

PHOTO 17. The outside-of-the-foot kick.

THE CHIP KICK

Sometimes it is necessary to lift a ground ball steeply into the air, such as when attempting to kick the ball over a nearby opponent to a teammate. In this situation the chip kick or chip shot is an effective way to move the ball precisely and neatly.

The kicking foot in photo 18 is turned outwards and hits underneath the ball in a

PHOTO 18. The chip kick.

scooping action. The body should lean backwards to give it the extra boost.

The chip kick resembles a golf chip shot; a short sharp swing. It is best used when the ball is either stationary or coming toward you. Forget about the chip shot when the ball is moving away from you; it's practically impossible.

THE BACK HEEL

Another kick you should not attempt when the ball is moving away is the back heel. This kick is best accomplished when the ball is level with or just in front of your kicking leg, allowing your leg to step over it so that the heel can hit it firmly on the back swing. It is effective when you are seeking to surprise your opponent when passing and can also be valuable when dribbling.

THE VOLLEY

So far we have concentrated on kicking ground balls, both stationary and moving. A more difficult task awaits the beginner when he begins to practice hitting balls arriving at different heights and varying speeds.

Although timing plays a much more im-

Here the instep is being used with the toe pointed down. The knee is well over the ball, as is the body, guaranteeing the ball's staying the same height all the way to its destination. If height had been desired the body would be leaning backwards and the kicking foot would be swinging up instead of through the ball.

When a ball comes at you waist-high you will have to turn your body sideways to enable the leg to move forward across the body to reach the ball. Photo 20 shows the sideways approach with the kicking leg ready to strike the ball with the instep.

Inside-of-the-Foot Volley

Often called the push volley, this kick is intended for short and accurate passing of the ball. It has little power, but because it has a short back swing it is easier to learn than the low or high volley kicks.

The Half Volley

Only through constant practice can this kick be learned, for more than any other it requires precise timing. The ball must be kicked just as it is rising and is one or two inches from the ground. If the ball is kicked just as it is bouncing the kick will probably result in a wild high ball; if it is hit when it has rebounded up more than a few inches it will be struck by the shin or knee and bounce out of control.

The half volley is kicked with the toe pointed and the knee and body over the ball as in the low instep kick. When hit like this the ball will travel faster and harder than with any other kick. To loft the ball it is simply a matter of remembering the principles for the lofted instep kick; adjusting the knee, the body, and the position of the nonkicking foot.

The Overhead Volley

A classic kick of modern soccer made popular by the South American pro-

PHOTO 19. The volley: make sure the toes are pointed down.

PHOTO 20. The sideways approach.

portant part, the volley and half volley are basically the same as the instep kick. The major difference is the height of the kicking leg when the ball is struck. Look at the ordinary volley demonstrated in photo 19.

PHOTO 21. A left-footed inside-of-the-foot volley by Wally Obrebski of the Chicago Sting. Note the short follow-through. (Photo—Bill Smith)

PHOTO 22. Wally Obrebski prepares for a half volley. He will kick the ball just as it is rising from the bounce. (Photo—Bill Smith)

head volley (also called the scissors or bicycle kick) is that the kicker's body must be lower than the foot at the time of contact—otherwise you wind up kicking the ball into your own face. To avoid any self-inflicted injuries, make certain the top part of your body drops to the ground as the ball is kicked. Photo 23 shows the outstretched hands ready to break the fall. Notice how the toes are pulled back toward the body in order to guide the ball over the player's head.

Incidentally, if an opponent is near and is trying to play the ball the referee may call "dangerous play." Most free kicks for dangerous play are given when a player tries to kick at a high ball (over chest-high) when another is attempting to head it, as shown in photo 24.

fessionals, the overhead volley is, unfortunately, overused in soccer today. It does, however, offer an attacker who is facing the wrong way the opportunity to surprise the defense with a shot at goal.

One of the main drawbacks of the over-

SHOOTING

When shooting (as in all kicking) remember to look at your target before you kick. Once you begin your kicking swing your eyes must be on the ball. Keep the body well over the ball and allow for a full follow-through.

Use the instep and the outside-of-the-foot kick for ground balls and the half volley for the higher balls. The overhead volley can also be used when facing away from the goal, and, of course, the head shot (header) for all balls coming higher than your chest.

You must have accuracy as well as power, so try aiming for the corners of the goal every time you shoot—and keep your shots low.

Always be prepared to kick quickly whenever the opportunity arises. A ball that comes to you in your opponent's penalty area must be hit the first time; don't try to trap it or control it.

PASSING

As I mentioned earlier, the inside-of-the-foot kick should be used for short low passes, though at times the outside-of-the-foot jab can be a safe substitute. For longer passes along the ground the instep is a must. For high passes use the lofted instep kick and for first-time clearances from the penalty area use the volley.

The main distinction between passing and shooting is the power put into the kick. Normally a pass is gentle and is designed so that your teammate will receive it when it is traveling at a pace that can be controlled. Ideally the pass should be aimed so that the player can run on to it without breaking his stride.

There are many coaches who prefer passes to be made directly to the player, while others desire to see the ball placed ahead of the receiver for the latter to run on to. Check with your coach to see if he has a preference. Personally, I advocate a mixture of both: to the man when he is stationary; ahead of him when running.

When passing directly to a teammate try to aim to whichever of his feet is the farthest away from his opponent. Your teammate will have a better chance to keep

PHOTO 23. A well-executed overhead volley.

the ball if he receives it with his body between the ball and his opponent.

After you have passed the ball don't stop and watch. Stay in contact with the man you have passed to. The closer you and your teammate are, the more options are opened to him.

When you receive a pass always run to meet it if possible; never wait for it to come to you, or your opponents will probably dart in between you and the ball to intercept it.

Accurate passing is more essential than ever in modern soccer, where maintaining possession of the ball has become the all-important factor. Your usefulness to your team will be greatly diminished if your passing is faulty, no matter how proficient you become in all other skills of soccer.

PHOTO 24. An obvious example of dangerous play.

PHOTO 25. Gordon Hill stops the ball dead with an inside-of-the-foot trap.
(Photo—Bill Smith)

chapter 4
BALL CONTROL

Making the ball do what you wish it to do is what ball control is all about. Whether it is plucking a high ball from the air with your feet, receiving a fast ball while on the run, or heading a goal, the first step in making the ball the servant and you the master is to learn how to stop a moving ball. This is called trapping in soccer.

TRAPPING

Many parts of the body are used to trap a ball, but whichever one is chosen the key to success is gentleness. Never allow your body to crash into a moving ball. Instead let the receiving area cushion the ball upon contact, thereby taking the pace off the ball.

Inside-of-the-Foot Trap

I cannot recommend this trap too highly; it should be used whenever possible, particularly on ground balls. As photo 25 shows, the foot is relaxed and is giving a little upon contact. Remember, the harder the ball comes to you the more your foot should give. Notice also in photo 25 how well balanced the player is with his arms held out from his body and his body leaning over the ball. I think it is wise for beginners to always exaggerate all these body actions until soccer skills are perfected.

The inside-of-the-foot trap is also most effective in trapping lofted balls, especially the ones that come at you below chest level. The trick in bringing down the ball is to drop the foot straight down to the ground as soon as it cushions the ball; the ball will then follow the direction of the foot and come to rest on the ground ready for your next move.

PHOTO 27. The sole-of-the-foot trap.

PHOTO 26. The Chicago Sting's midfielder, Rudy Getzinger, brings down a high ball with an inside-of-the-foot trap. (Photo—Bill Smith)

The Sole-of-the-Foot Trap

As the name suggests, the ball is stopped by the sole of the foot, which acts as a wedge against the ball and the ground. Here again the foot must be relaxed. Use the sole trap whenever the ball is too far away or bouncing erratically to get to it with the inside-of-the-foot trap. But use it sparingly, for, unlike the inside-of-the-foot trap (where the player can move off with the ball immediately), everything stops momentarily when the foot is resting on top of the ball.

PHOTO 28. The outside-of-the-foot trap.

PHOTO 29. Eyes on the ball, Denny Vaninger, the St. Louis Stars and U.S. national team striker, controls the ball with a thigh trap.

The Outside-of-the-Foot Trap

This trap is most effective in controlling dropping balls. The foot and leg are turned toward the ground and with one quick flicking action the ball is smothered and stopped dead. As your trapping skills improve you will find that a gentle push after trapping will enable you to run off in the direction of the trapping foot.

The Thigh Trap

Another way to kill dropping balls is to use the thigh trap. The leg is raised with the knee bent and the ball strikes the middle part of the thigh just above the kneecap. Upon contact the thigh relaxes and the ball drops to the ground gently.

PHOTO 30. A perfect example of the chest trap by the talented George Ley of the Dallas Tornado. He is leaning back and his arms are held wide to avoid touching the high ball.

PHOTO 31. Another U.S. national team member of the St. Louis Stars, Al Trost, shows how to use the chest for balls coming straight at you.

The Chest Trap

Any ball higher than the waist and lower than the neck should be trapped with the chest. As with the foot and the thigh, the chest must give a little on impact. The arms should be held away from the body and the chest should be leaning backwards for a high ball (photo 30) or forward for a lower ball (photo 31). The ball is then guided down to the ground for the player's feet to take over.

HEADING

Heading the ball is not as difficult or as painful as it may appear to the beginner. He will probably learn to excel at heading long before he has mastered the other basic skills of soccer as long as he keeps in mind the three golden rules of heading:

1. Always keep your eye on the ball.
2. Always use the forehead.
3. Always strike the ball (don't let it strike you).

"Keep your eye on the ball" is a phrase you will hear time and time again in soccer, but at no time is this advice of more importance than when heading. A miscalculation of a few inches and, instead of the strongest part of the skull—the forehead—striking the ball, the sensitive and at times fragile nose could well be the painful point of contact. So make sure those eyes are open, at least until you strike the ball. Most players' eyes close for a fraction of a second upon contact, a natural reflex action.

For a clear illustration of the forehead in action, look at photo 32. Being flat, the forehead is able to give accurate direction to the ball when used correctly. The power behind the thrust comes from the tense neck muscles and the swing of the upper torso.

When heading, the upper torso is bent backwards and the knees are slightly bent; then as the trunk swings forward the forehead punches the ball powerfully. After contact the knees straighten out to add impetus to the heading action.

Timing becomes critical when jumping to head a ball. A lofty spring with either a one- or a two-legged jump-off will be of little value if you arrive too early or too late. The jump header has more power than the standing header, the extra power coming from the thrust of the moving body, particularly when the body jackknifes in midair. When jumping, try to reach as high as or higher than the ball so that you can then push the forehead across or down into the ball, depending on what type of header is desired.

Head the ball downwards when aiming for the goal; most goalies have trouble with the low header. Heading upwards is usually reserved for defenders clearing their line. To head sideways or backwards, simply turn the forehead in the desired direction and use the same body and neck action as you used in the jump header.

PHOTO 32. Rod Johnson of the Chicago Sting makes perfect contact with the ball. (Photo— Bill Smith)

PHOTO 33. With "King" Pele and Kyle Rote, Jr. (12) close by, Bobby Moffat of the Dallas Tornado heads sideways. (Photo— Raff Frano)

TACKLING

Tackling is far different in soccer from what we understand it to be in football. There are no body checks, holding, or pushing in soccer tackling; only the feet can be used. Photo 34 shows the front block tackle, the most often used tackle in soccer. As in all other tackles you should get close to your opponent before committing yourself. Both of your feet should be balanced, and your tackling foot takes all the weight of your body, so that the tackling foot will not be damaged if it is kicked by your opponent but will simply be pushed back under pressure.

Notice also in photo 34 that the opponents' shoulders have come in contact with each other. This is legal as long as it is shoulder against shoulder—there will be more about shoulder charging later.

Side Block Tackle

Sometimes it is not possible to face your opponent when tackling. In this situation

PHOTO 34. The front block tackle.

the side block or sliding tackle is used. Very similar to the front block tackle, the side block tackle requires that you pivot on your standing foot as you approach from the side. Try to get as close as possible to your opponent so that there is power behind your tackle.

Slide Tackle

Like the overhead volley kick, the sliding tackle is another soccer skill that should be used when no other course of action is feasible. I call it the "desperation tackle," since it is usually seen in moments of panic when a defender has to gamble to save the day. If he connects, the sliding tackle can be a thing of beauty, one of the most exciting moments in soccer; if he fails, he is left floundering on the ground while his opponent moves on unmolested.

The object of this tackle is not simply to stop the ball but to kick it away from your opponent. The tackling foot is used in a short swinging motion so that the inside of the foot strikes the ball. The standing leg begins to bend and, along with the hand on the same side of the body, takes the weight of the impending fall. The slide tackle is best performed on a wet field. One of the best slide tacklers I've seen is Clive Griffiths of the Chicago Sting.

Shoulder Charging

As we noted before, the shoulder charge is legal as long as shoulder hits shoulder. Although it is the only form of intentional body contact permitted in soccer, you can still find yourself being penalized by the referee for charging too violently.

For a fair shoulder charge, the ball must be within playing distance; the hand and arms must not be employed to elbow or push the opponent; and, above all, the point of contact has to be shoulder against shoulder.

PHOTO 35. Mike England (5) of the Seattle Sounders is too late with his side block tackle as Art Welch of the San Jose Earthquakes connects with a hard shot.

PHOTO 36. The slide tackle performed by Richard Green of the Chicago Sting. (Photo—Bill Smith)

PHOTO 37. The shoulder charge.

Shoulder charging is used to best advantage when attempting to knock a player off the ball when running alongside him. The best time to use it is when your opponent is balancing on his outside leg. Of course, you must expect your opponent to be ready to do the same to you, so remember to lean into him when being tackled.

DRIBBLING

Of all the varied soccer skills to be learned, none can give more enjoyment to the player than dribbling. Mastering the art of manipulating a ball from one foot to the other at varying speeds through and around opponents is a thrill that can only be equalled by the scoring of a goal.

To confuse, elude, and surprise is the goal of a top dribbler, and the tools he uses are the feint, acceleration, change of pace, and of course ball control.

Controlling the ball while dribbling consists of soft strokes with the inside and the outside of the instep. The foot is turned out slightly to allow the inside of the instep to come in contact with the ball. For optimum balance lean slightly over the ball and place your weight on the balls of your feet when dribbling at slow speeds.

The feint can include the use of hips, shoulder, and legs to make your opponents go the wrong way. Some of the more popular feints are:

1. As your opponent draws near you, lean to the right, swaying from the waist with the shoulder leaning out, then push the ball to the left.

2. Thrust your right foot over and across the ball. The foot's movement should be enough to make your opponent veer toward it. When this happens, push the ball to your right with a gentle touch of your left foot and move off.

3. With your opponent running alongside you, step on the ball with the sole of the foot, then turn and run in the opposite direction.

4. Tempt your opponent by moving the ball close to him. When he makes a lunge for it, pull the ball back with the sole of the foot and run off in a different direction.

Along with the feint, acceleration and change of pace play a vital part in dribbling. Once the opponent is left off balance, the dribbler must move off quickly and capitalize on the space created.

Quite often simply approaching an opponent at half speed, then accelerating when you get close to him, will enable you to get past him.

PHOTO 38. Ian Moore, the Chicago Sting's winger, has his foot turned outward as he dribbles up to his opponent. (Photo—Bill Smith)

PHOTO 39. Rudy Getzinger shows the ball, hoping his opponent will make a lunge for it. (Photo—Bill Smith)

PHOTO 40. Perfectly balanced, the "wizard of dribble," Gordon Hill, tricks his way through a packed defense. (Photo—Bill Smith)

When dribbling at slow speeds keep the ball close to your feet; but when dribbling at top speeds keep the ball two or three feet ahead of you so that you do not have to break your stride while running.

A word of caution about dribbling: never dribble when a pass will do. Unless you are a genius like Pele don't try beating two or three opponents. It might work occasionally, but most of the time you will lose the ball, and even if you don't, unless you're running directly toward the goal with the ball your opponents will have time to reorganize and regroup.

RUNNING WITH THE BALL

There is a difference between running and dribbling. In soccer, running with the ball assumes the player is running unmolested, whereas in dribbling he is running while trying to evade or trick an opponent. Therefore, running with the ball is more a matter of controlling the ball at high speeds. This is best accomplished by turning in the toes so that the ball is tapped with the outside of the foot as the foot touches the ground.

The secret of good ball control while running is to take short steps and keep the arms wide of your body. Better balance is obtained this way, enabling the runner to change directions at will, or if necessary, to feint or stop quickly. Even a sudden reverse can be accomplished at high speeds when using short steps. Try to look ahead of the ball when running so that you can see the approach of opponents.

RUNNING WITHOUT THE BALL

Nearly as important as running with the ball is running without it (also called running off the ball) in support of your teammates. I expect to see all of my team moving, the player with the ball and the others, either jogging as they wait for a chance to break or running into an open space for a pass. Without their support the player with the ball will have little option but to either dribble or shoot, but with teammates around him his alternatives multiply.

Anyone who gets the opportunity to see as many first-division games in England and Germany as I do will be struck at once by the tremendous movement off the ball—much more than in the NASL or in other foreign countries. Since it is commonly accepted that the English and German first divisions are the strongest pro leagues in the world, one could well argue that it is the amount of movement off the ball that makes the difference.

PHOTO 41. Chicago Sting defender John Webb prepares to tap the ball with his right foot as he advances down the field. Note the toes, turned inward. (Photo—Bill Smith)

PHOTO 42. Ian Moore looks around for opponents without breaking his stride. (Photo—Bill Smith)

PHOTO 43. Both running with and without the ball are graphically illustrated in this photo as Miami Toros' Estaban Aranguiz moves at top speed with the ball while his teammate Ronnie Sharp runs into a supporting position. (Photo—John Pineda)

SCREENING

One other technique that plays a vital part in ball control is screening. The farther away you can keep your opponent from the ball and the less you let him see of it, the more chance you have of keeping possession. The main point to remember is to control the ball with the foot farthest away from your opponent. To make it even more difficult for him to get at the ball, use the outside of your foot whenever possible. Photo 44 clearly shows the problem the defender has trying to get near the ball without resorting to pushing or committing some other violation.

Work hard on improving your ball control. The great Pele, even at this stage of his career, spends up to two hours a day practicing his.

PHOTO 44. Rudy Getzinger screens the ball with his body.
(Photo—Bill Smith)

PHOTO 48. Merv Cawston of the Chicago Sting pulls the ball into his chest as he saves a chest-high ball. (Photo—Bill Smith)

chapter 5
THE GOALKEEPER

Goalies come in all sizes but preferably they should be within the five-ten to six-foot range. The buffeting they must withstand in the goalmouth is best handled by strong goalies. Although there have been exceptions, lack of reach has unhappily stopped many agile and safe goalkeepers from attaining top-class status.

I have found that basketball players make the transition to soccer goalkeeping with ease. Having a "safe" pair of hands is, of course, the major requirement: catching the ball is always preferable to punching or deflecting it away. Another valuable attribute for a goalie is agility: jumping, diving, and falling have to be accomplished at split-second speed.

The three points all new goalies should memorize are:

1. Keep the body behind the ball.
2. Keep the eyes on the ball.
3. Catch the ball whenever possible.

The goalkeeper is the one specialist in soccer. His world is not one of dribbling, tackling, heading, and most of the other soccer skills. Instead, it includes positioning, anticipation, catching, punching, diving, and throwing. Kicking is the only skill he shares in common with the rest of the team, and even this is usually limited to goal kicks and punts.

The goalie is expected to be completely in charge of his goal area. Any ball that comes into the 20- by 6-yard box should be his, and he should have a clear understanding about this with the rest of his defense. He must also be prepared to shout out instructions to his colleagues: when he yells, "It's mine!" the rest of the defense must let the ball go through to him. Another of his responsibilities is to run out of goal and confront any attacker who breaks through unopposed.

Quite often the only way to stop the advancing opponent is to dive at his feet and clutch the ball. At other times, particularly when the attacker is chasing a long through pass, the goalie must race him to the ball and kick it away.

The modern goalie is not only an integral part of the defense but has also become an important cog in the offensive machinery. Many goals come from the initial pass out of the goal area to a defender beginning a series of passes that ends with a striker scoring down at the other end of the field. But despite the new offensive-minded breed of goalkeepers, the major task for a goalkeeper is to stop the ball going into his own net.

GROUND BALLS

Balls coming straight at you are best dealt with by going down on one knee. Keep your weight on the non-kneeling leg so that if the ball bounces awkwardly you won't be immobile. The fingers of the hand should be spread open and the palms upwards. When the ball is gathered, pull it up to the chest for added protection against an unexpected collision.

Another way to field low balls is to simply stand in the path of the ball with both legs together as in photo 46. The advantage here is that a bad bounce can be handled better than when you are on one knee. The disadvantage is that a fierce shot is very difficult to hold onto in this posi-

PHOTO 45. Watch out for the bad bounce.

tion. I suggest beginners use this method for weak shots and get down on the knee for the hard ones.

WAIST AND CHEST-HIGH BALLS

Always use the stomach or chest for support when catching waist or chest-high balls. Photos 47 and 48 show why. The stomach and chest form perfect shields so that even if you fail to catch the ball or mishandle it, your body will bar the way to goal. Upon impact the ball is pulled into your stomach or chest—which should be relaxed, thereby cushioning the shot.

HIGH BALLS

The ideal way to field the high ball is to catch it. This is easier said than done in a crowded goal area with challenging opponents obstructing your path or attempting to head the ball before you can reach it.

PHOTO 46. Make sure the legs are together.

PHOTO 47. Cushioning a waist-high ball.

Photo 49 is a good illustration of a goalie catching under pressure. Notice the goalie's hands held behind the ball and his eyes on the ball. As soon as the catch is made the ball is brought down to the chest.

PUNCHING AND DEFLECTING

For safety's sake many high balls must be punched away or deflected over the bar. If possible try and punch with two hands. This gives added power. Start your swing with your arms bent, straightening them out at the point of impact. A further safety measure is to punch the ball in the same direction as it came.

Sometimes the high ball comes so close to the crossbar or the upright that punching it might mean a broken hand. In this situation the upper part of the palm of the hand is used to deflect the ball either over or around the posts. Here again exact timing is vital. Do not get into the habit of using the back of the hand to deflect the ball, for quite often the ball will bounce off the knuckles in the direction that might well embarass you: into your own goal.

DIVING SAVES

The best advice I can give to any goalie is never dive unless it is an emergency. All too

PHOTO 49. Peter ("The Cat") Bonetti of the St. Louis Stars soars to pull down a high ball.

PHOTO 50. A good deflection with the palm of the hand.

many good goalkeepers fail to make it to the top because of their insistence on making spectacular dives to field simple shots that could have been reached by taking a step or two. Of course, there are occasions when goalies have to dive to reach well-placed shots. When this happens the body once again must be behind the incoming ball, to act as the secondary shield. The ball can be either caught or punched, but if it is caught it must then be brought into the chest and hugged. For a safe landing the leg closest to the ground, the buttocks, and the upper arm act to break the fall.

DIVING AT AN OPPONENT

As I mentioned earlier, sometimes only a courageous dive at an opponent's feet will save the day. Whenever a forward comes through alone the goalie must move quickly to cut him off. He should dive at the ball

PHOTO 51. In a stretching dive when the body is unable to get behind the ball, care must be taken that the ball is quickly pulled into the stomach after it has been caught.

with his body forming as large an obstacle as possible to the ball. Care should be taken that he is not tricked by the opponent, who may feint to go one way and then go the other.

NARROWING THE ANGLE

Diagram E shows clearly why a goalie must come out of his goal when an opponent breaks through alone. This narrowing of the angle is a must; not only does it give less of a target for the opponent to aim for but it will also compel him to shoot from farther out.

ANTICIPATION AND POSITIONING

There's an old adage in soccer that great goalies are waiting for the ball to arrive while ordinary goalies are running, jumping, or diving to get at it. This still holds true. Very seldom do you see top-flight goalies diving full length for a ball; instead, they appear to have a sixth sense, seemingly directing the shot or header toward their waiting hands.

Anticipation is best mastered by actual match-play experience. The first important step is getting to know the style of play of your own defenders so that you can judge with reasonable assurance what each of them will do in a given situation. Learning something about your opponents is the next step. Find out which of the opposing team members usually score the goals, which ones favor their right foot, and who, if any, are good in the air. Finally, always expect the unexpected: miskicks, deflections, or poorly placed passes back to you from a desperate teammate—nothing should come as a surprise.

As in narrowing the angle, positioning is also a geometric problem that each goalkeeper must solve. Where to stand so that the least amount of goal is offered as a target is all a matter of angles. A good rule of thumb is to stand on the right side of the goal, a few feet out from the right goal post, for all attacking movements coming from your right; the opposite side of the goal, of

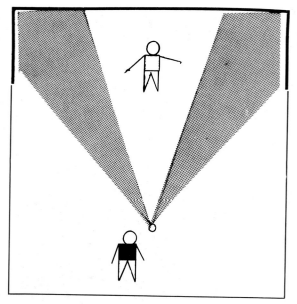
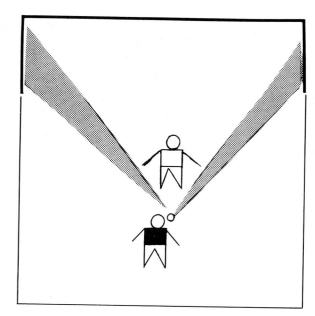

DIAGRAM E. NARROWING THE ANGLE.

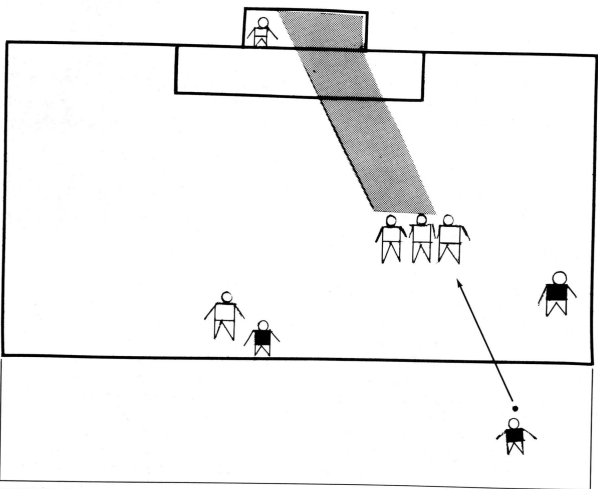

DIAGRAM F. FORMING A WALL.
Shaded area protected by wall.

course, for those coming from the left; and in the center of your goal if the attack shifts toward the center of your goal.

For corner kicks, always stand at the far post (the post farthest away from the position of the ball) so that you can make your move after you see how far the kick will go. If you were to take up a position by the near post it would mean having to run backwards to chase the ball should it be kicked over your head.

FORMING A DEFENSIVE WALL

On all free kicks near the goal, the defense should form a wall of three, four, or more players. The fundamental aim of the human wall is to cover one side of the goal (always the side closest to the ball), thereby leaving a smaller area of responsibility for the goalie. In diagram F the usual arrangement is shown. Naturally, if the ball should be lofted over the wall, spun around the wall, or sent through the wall, it's up to the goalkeeper to try to reach it.

KICKING AND THROWING

Kicking for goalies means goal kicks and punts. Goal kicks are kicked inside the edge of the goal area and the ball must go out of the penalty area to be in play. If the ball does not pass out of the penalty area, the kick must be retaken. Quite often goal kicks are taken by some other defender, normally the man with the strongest kick, but whoever the kicker is he should employ the basic lofted instep kick.

When kicking a punt volley the ball should be held out away from the body. There should be a full back swing of the kicking leg; the instep should be firm and the follow-through overemphasized. Although long punts downfield are only a 50-50 proposition when it comes to maintaining possession, there are times when a good hefty clearance into the opponent's

PHOTO 52. The bowling throw.

half can result in a fast breakaway.

The three standard throws in soccer are the bowling, the overarm, and the javelin.

The bowling throw has a great advantage: the ball arrives at the teammate's feet on the ground, ready for him to run with it. The overarm (thrown over the head) and the javelin (thrown at head level), on the other hand, although capable of attaining much longer distances (some goalies can reach the halfway line with the overarm throw), usually require the receiver to stop to trap the ball. Whatever throw is chosen, never throw to a

PHOTO 53. The overarm throw.

teammate who is closely guarded, for above all a goalkeeper's motto must be "safety first."

CARRYING THE BALL

The law states that the goalkeeper must release the ball after carrying it four steps. If you carry it five or more steps without re-leasing it, an indirect free kick will be awarded to your opponents. Goalkeepers circumvent this rule by dropping the ball to the ground after four steps, then picking it up again for another four steps. If you do this too often, however, the referee will award a free kick against you for wasting time.

PHOTO 54. The javelin throw.

WEATHER

The weather affects the goalkeeper more than other members of the team. Windy days can make high balls swerve, curve, and drop surprisingly; rainy days can cause slick, slippery balls.

Goalkeepers must be especially alert on windy days when defending from corner kicks and high volley shots.

On wet days watch out for the ball's tendency to bounce through instead of up. It is essential for a goalkeeper to wear gloves whenever the field is wet.

PHOTO 55. The perfect penalty. Estaban Aranguiz of the Miami Toros sends the ball into the low corner. Note how the goalie has tried unsuccessfully to anticipate the direction of the ball.

chapter 6
THE DEAD BALL

The thoughtful use of the dead ball is a vital part of tactical soccer and is the one time where prematch plans should be employed. From the humblest grade school eleven to the top professional squads, every team should have a variety of set plays in which to exploit the temporary advantage of having uncontested possession of the ball at such times as throw-ins, goal kicks, free kicks, and corner kicks.

When is the ball dead? Any time the ball goes completely over the goal line or touchline (sideline) and whenever the referee blows his whistle for an infraction. A throw-in is given when the ball goes over the touchline and is taken by the team opposite to the one last touching the ball before it went over the line. A goal kick is awarded when the offensive team last touches the ball and a corner kick when it is the defensive team who last touches the ball prior to its crossing the goal line.

THROW-INS

The rule applying to throw-ins states that the ball must be thrown with both hands over the head and with both feet on or outside the touchline. Both of the feet must be on the ground and the thrower must be facing the field when throwing. The power from the throw-in comes with the final thrust of the arms and the shifting of weight from the rear to the front leg.

To throw a "long ball" more emphasis is placed on bending the back from the waist before throwing, then straightening it with a whiplike swing. Some players can throw up to forty yards in this manner.

The main thing to keep in mind about throw-ins is to take them quickly. Surprise and advantage will often come from a quickly taken throw when your opposition has not had time to cover your teammates.

If possible, throw down toward your teammate's feet so that he can quickly get the ball under control. If he is closely guarded he can always push it right back to you with the inside of the foot.

For the more intricate throws the options are, of course, unlimited. In diagram G, for instance, the thrower could aim for the space to the side of either of his two teammates. He could then run into the

space vacated by them for the return pass.

The long throw is best employed in the opponent's half, especially if the thrower can reach the opponent's goalmouth. Diagram H shows a much-used long throw in professional soccer. The ball is not thrown into the crowded goalmouth, the most obvious place, but is directed at a nearby teammate, whose task it is to head it on to another teammate positioned near the goal.

In your own half of the field it is always a good idea to throw the ball back to the goalkeeper if there are no unguarded teammates nearby. However, it is most unwise to throw the ball to a teammate in the direction of your own goal; an interception by an opponent or a teammate's slipping to

DIAGRAM G. Thrower A receives pass in shaded area from either B or C.

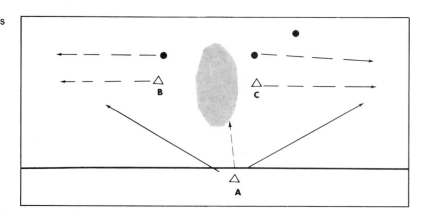

DIAGRAM H. THE LONG THROW.

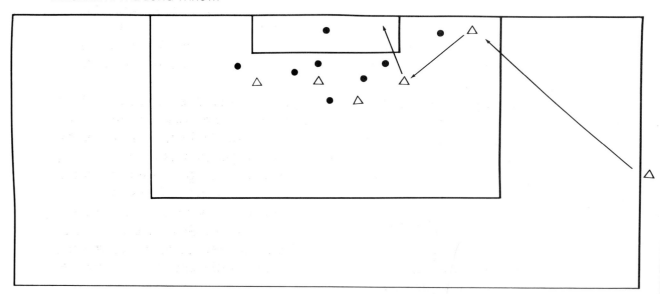

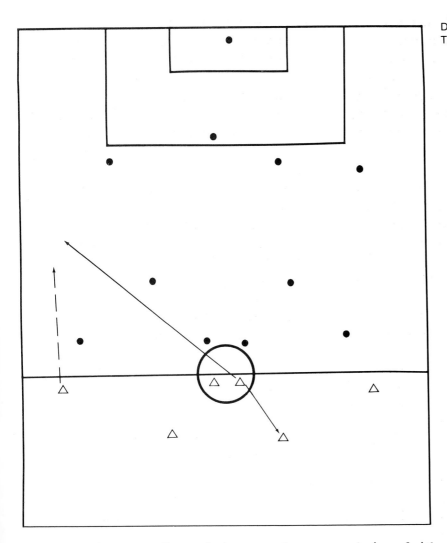

DIAGRAM I.
THE KICKOFF.

the ground may well result in a goal—against you.

When defending against a throw-in every opponent in range must be quickly covered. The closer you stand to your opponent the less chance he will have to control the ball before you challenge him. Always stand behind your opponent, never in front of him. If you forget to do this, the ball will most certainly be thrown over your head and your opponents will be off running free with the ball.

KICKOFFS

Kickoffs occur on three occasions in soccer:

1. At the beginning of the game—the team who wins the toss has the choice of either kicking off or picking which direction the team will play.

2. At the beginning of the second half—this time taken by the team that did not kick off in the first half.

3. After each goal is scored—the team being scored against taking it.

A kickoff is an indirect free kick, which means the player who kicks it cannot touch it again until the ball has been played by some other player from either team. Also, as we noted earlier, a goal cannot be scored directly from an indirect free kick.

Diagram I shows some of the ways a team can kick off. Since the ball is not played until the referee blows his whistle, there is very little chance for surprise.

Rather, it is a time to maintain possession until the ball can be moved down to the opponent's penalty area. The ball out to the winger is one way, and the pass back to the midfieldman another. In both instances the aim is to get as many players as possible into the opponent's penalty area before the long pass is sent. Some teams prefer a slower build-up from the kickoff, passing short passes among themselves as they try to entice opponents away from their penalty area. Whether it is the fast breakaway or a slower attack approach, keeping possession should be the basic strategy underlying all kickoffs.

FREE KICKS

Unlike the kickoff, goals can (and do) come from quickly taken free kicks. If possible, you should take your free kicks before the opposition can organize itself. A short pass to an unguarded teammate often results in a shot at goal. Unfortunately, you will probably find a human wall of defenders formed as soon as a free kick is awarded and—unless your opponents are inexperienced—every one of your teammates closely guarded. But even in these tight situations there are ways of infiltrating the defense and beating the wall. Diagrams J and K suggest some profitable methods.

Since in every free kick situation the opposing team must be at least ten yards from the ball, it is clear that the kicking team should exploit this by having one or more players waiting for a pass within the empty ten-yard radius. Diagram L shows a typical ploy. Player X, who has a better view of the goal, is waiting for the short pass from B. This play is most important for indirect free kicks since as I mentioned earlier a goal cannot be scored directly from the kick.

Another way to beat the wall is to chip the ball over or curve it around the wall. The outside-of-the-foot kick is used to make the ball swerve around the wall. Sometimes called the banana shot, this kick is accomplished by hitting the ball off center, which makes the ball spin violently. The superstar of American soccer, Pele, scores many goals this way.

DIAGRAM J. BEATING THE WALL. Kicker A chips the ball over the wall for either B, C, D, or E to chase in drop zone.

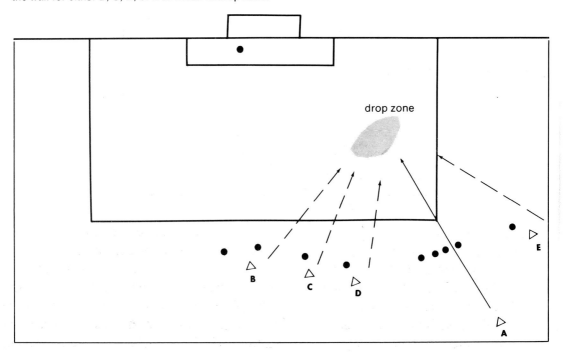

DIAGRAM K. BEATING THE WALL BY DRAWING THE DEFENSE AWAY FROM THE DROP ZONE.

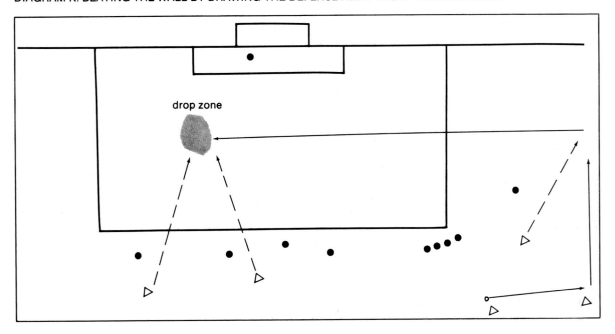

DIAGRAM L. INDIRECT FREE KICK.

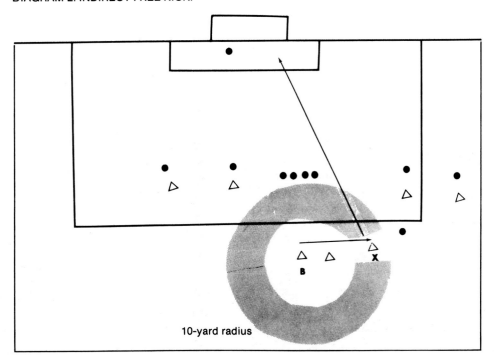

In defending against a free kick, all defenders should move as close as possible to their nearest opponents. If the infringement is near the goal line, then of course a wall must be formed quickly, while midfieldmen and even strikers rush back to help maintain numerical superiority. The goalkeeper must direct the wall's formation so that he can see the ball at all times.

One other point to keep in mind with indirect free kicks concerns infractions that take place ten yards or less from the goal line. In this situation the defenders are permitted to line up on the goal line to protect their goal despite the ten-yard rule governing all free kicks.

PENALTY KICKS

When a penalty kick is awarded, none of the defenders are permitted inside the penalty area other than the goalkeeper. The same rule applies to all the attackers except the player elected to kick the penalty. There is little that can be said about penalties; at a distance of only twelve yards the kicker should score. I prefer to have my players shoot the ball low, aiming for one of the corners, with emphasis on accuracy rather than power. Kicking the ball as hard as you can is one of the reasons players miss scoring from penalty kicks.

As for the goalkeeper, there is not much he can do other than guess which way the kicker will shoot. Since a goalie must stand still on his goal line until his opponent has kicked, many goalies take a chance and dive either to the right or left at the same time the kick is taken. This reduces the odds to an even-money risk.

As soon as the penalty kick is taken, all other players may come back into the penalty area. This can be important if the ball rebounds off the crossbar or post, for as in all other free kicks, the penalty kicker cannot touch the ball again until someone else plays it.

THE OFFSIDE TRAP

Watch out for the offside trap when taking free kicks. As I noted in Chapter Two, when the ball is played to the attacking player there must be two defenders between him and the goal line. Diagram M shows the offside trap, which many teams employ during free kicks. Many attackers in their excitement to receive a pass from the free kick forget to watch the movement of defenders, making the defenders' task that much simpler.

The offside trap, however, can be a dangerous tactic if used too often. The attackers, expecting the trap, will often move backwards with the defenders thus nullifying it; and even worse, you cannot

DIAGRAM M. OFFSIDE TRAP. A, B, and C move forward just before Z takes free kick.

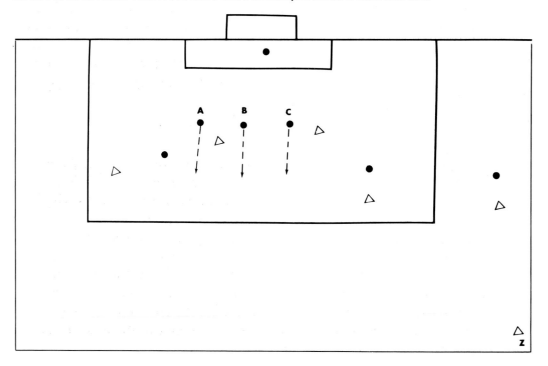

DIAGRAM N. CORNER KICK INTO SHADED AREA.

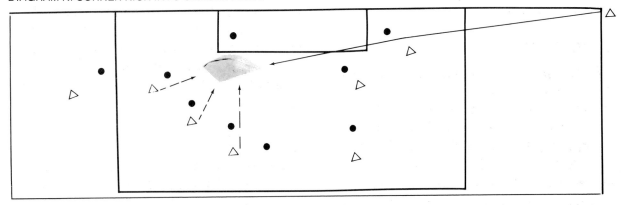

DIAGRAM O. SHORT CORNER KICK.

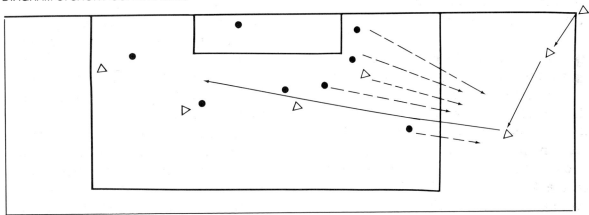

always rely upon the referee's or the linesmen's catching the offside infringement amid the hurried movement of players.

CORNER KICKS

Most corner kicks are hit high into the goalmouth for tall strikers to reach with their heads. The place to aim for is the area around the penalty spot, far enough away from the goal so that the goalie will not come out to intercept the ball.

As in diagram N, some forwards deliberately leave a space near the goal into which the ball can be kicked. Then as the ball approaches they make a run into the space to meet the ball. Another method is the short corner, which, as diagram O shows, can open up the packed defense by drawing some of the defenders away from the goalmouth toward the corner flag.

In taking corner kicks a winger should be able to kick both the outswinger and the inswinger. The outswinger is kicked with the right foot from the right wing, and the inswinger is taken with the left foot from the right wing. On the left wing, the opposite feet are used.

DROP BALLS

Whenever play is stopped for any reason other than infringements of the rules, such as a serious injury or the referee's wishing to consult a linesman, the restart takes the form of a drop ball between one player from each team with everyone else ten yards away. The ball is in play as soon as it touches the ground. Unlike the other restarts, there is little tactical or strategic advantage to either team at the time of a drop ball.

PHOTO 56. Passing in a crowded penalty area.

chapter 7
OFFENSIVE SOCCER

Although many of us would like to think getting exercise while having fun is what soccer is all about, the truth is, of course, that the object of the game is to score goals. How to get the ball in the back of your opponent's net should be on everyone's mind, even your defenders. Every time your team is in possession, your team is attacking; the goalkeeper, defenders, midfieldmen, all of them must think of themselves as attackers. Through a series of passes, running off the ball, and interchanging positions, the ball can be moved from one goal to the other.

But to get to the opposite goal requires some form of team plan, not set plays but rather a general understanding as to what is required from each player.

TEAM FORMATIONS

Looking at the different formations of modern soccer can give some indication of the players' responsibilities when attacking. In diagram P the basic formations are shown with arrows depicting the area of general responsibility for each player.

Of all the modern soccer formations in vogue today, I recommend the 4-3-3 (four defenders, three midfielders, and three attackers—the goalie is never shown when discussing formations since his position remains constant). Ideally, the 4-3-3 should enable you to have seven men in defense and six in attack if the midfieldmen can do the amount of running required. Com-

DIAGRAM P.

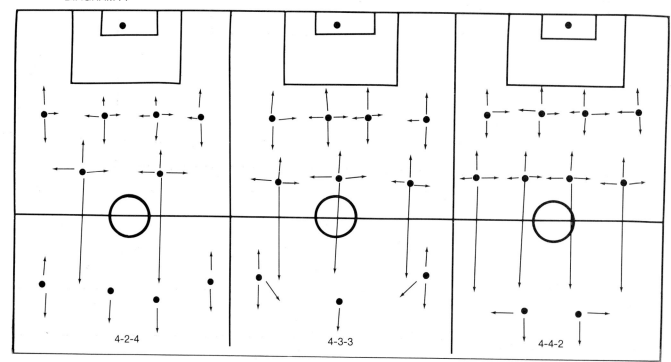

4-2-4   4-3-3   4-4-2

pared to this the 4-2-4 can only give six men in defense and six in attack, and with only two midfielders it is obviously weaker in the vital midfield area than the 4-3-3.

Another formation, the 4-4-2, is used by many defense-minded professional teams. In this system the lack of attackers is supposedly offset by the four midfieldmen and one or two of the outside backs' moving forward as necessary, but most of the teams that play 4-4-2 are weak ones trying to hold their opponents to a 0-0 tie. I see no reason why a beginner should involve himself with this purely negative system.

There are many people in soccer today who also think the 4-3-3 is too defensive; I don't. As long as your three midfieldmen are creative as well as strong there is no reason why your team playing 4-3-3 cannot beat any playing 4-2-4. The strength of 4-3-3 is the happy balance between a strong defense and a strong attack made possible by the mobility and support of the three midfieldmen. Everyone on attack when in possession and everyone on defense when

possession is lost is the basis of successful 4-3-3.

ATTACK IN DEPTH

With everyone in support, a wide variety of options are opened up to the player in possession, but care must be taken that the supporting teammates are not strung out in a straight line where they can be drawn into an offside position and where too many lateral passes are made. Passing across instead of through not only makes it easier for opponents to intercept but also ignores the purpose of an attack: penetration.

As can be seen in diagram Q, an attack in depth offers many more possibilities, both for triangular and reverse inter-passing and also for creating that most vital element in soccer: space.

MAKING SPACE

Attackers should always be searching for space, that open unguarded area in which a pass can be either placed or received.

DIAGRAM Q.
ATTACK IN DEPTH.

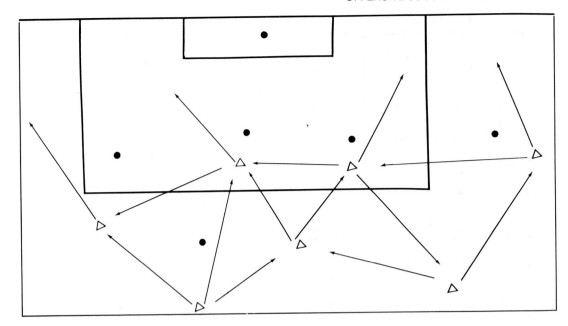

DIAGRAM R. EXISTING SPACE.
X passes ball into shaded area
for either A, B, or C to collect.

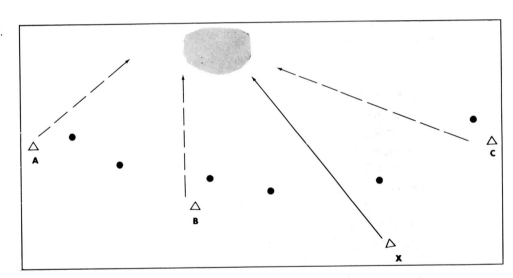

DIAGRAM S. CREATING
SPACE. A moves to the right,
taking opponent S with him. B
then moves across to accept
pass from X.

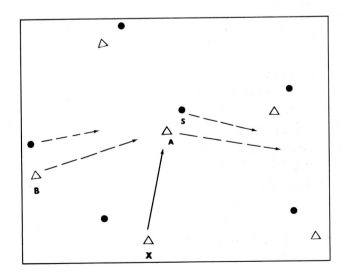

Naturally the closer you get to your opponent's goal the harder it will be to find an open area, but it can be done. There are two ways of making space: utilizing existing space as in diagram R, and creating space so that defenders are lured away from a particular area into which a pass can be sent to another teammate (diagram S).

ATTACK IN WIDTH

As we will note in the next chapter, modern defenses tend to congregate in front of their penalty areas. Because of this, attacks should not be restricted to one flank or one area. Cross-passing across the complete width of the field is one way of spreading the defense, as is fast penetration down the wings. Once the defense has been spread out, the gaps can be exploited by midfieldmen moving up or strikers interchanging their positions. In addition, the outside backs have an opportunity to move up along the wings and surprise the defense. In diagram T the right back is able success-

fully to overlap while the opposing defense's attention is focused on the left flank. The Chicago Sting's talented outside back, John Webb, is often seen racing down the wing overlapping his strikers.

MOBILITY

The players on attack can maintain added pressure on the opposing defense by continually moving into different positions and interchanging with their colleagues. This is where running off the ball plays such an important role in soccer: sprinting to pick up a pass; laying off the ball to a teammate and then running off again; taking a defender with you as you open up space; sprinting again to take another pass—on and on it goes. It's exhausting, but without this mobility the 4-3-3 attack would flounder for lack of support.

PASSING

In the final analysis a team's offense is only

DIAGRAM T. THE OVERLAP.

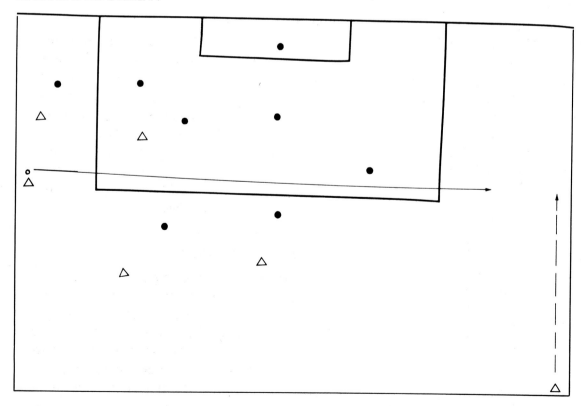

as good as its passing. Soccer, after all, is a passing game, and without proficiency in this fundamental technique neither an individual nor a team can expect to score many goals.

The most effective pass is the one that surprises your opponents, so vary your passes; don't stick with short ones, for instance. Mix up your high ones with ground passes, too. Certainly, the short ground pass is the safest and most accurate way to maintain possession, and no one will argue that the long high ball is easier for the opposing defense to reach, but without variety your passes will soon be anticipated by your opponents.

Surprise is also gained by disguising the direction of the pass, and one of the basic moves in soccer is passing the ball in the opposite direction from which you are running.

Let's look at some other passes that are designed to open up the defense:

The Wall Pass

Another basic move in soccer, the wall pass is used on 2-on-1 situations to go past the defender without having to dribble. As diagram U shows, the man with the ball (A) has passed to his teammate (B), who, acting as the wall, has returned the ball back to A. Surprise here has been achieved by A's running on the blind side of the defender for the return pass while the defender's attention has been focused on B.

DIAGRAM U. THE WALL PASS.

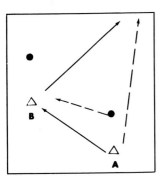

The Scissors Pass

Two players run across each other's path in this movement in an attempt to disguise their intentions. Either the player in possession or his teammate can move by the defender with the ball; in most cases, however, the player nearest the defender acts as the decoy, as in diagram V.

DIAGRAM V. THE SCISSORS PASS. B takes the ball away from A when they meet. A continues to run as if he still has the ball.

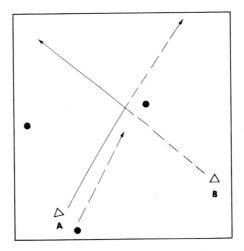

The Decoy Pass

As in the scissors pass, the intention here is to conceal from the defender which player will emerge with the ball. Any number of teammates can be employed in the decoy pass, but in diagram W only three are shown. Whatever the number, the idea is to have your teammates running past the man in possession, all calling for the ball—then another teammate who has been moving up unmolested receives the pass.

The Break-Reverse Pass

Probably the simplest pass to perfect, the break-reverse involves some sort of signal between the passer and receiver, usually a hand or finger motion, so that the passer knows which way the receiver intends to go. Once they understand each other, it's simply a matter of the receiver's running

DIAGRAM W.
THE DECOY PASS.

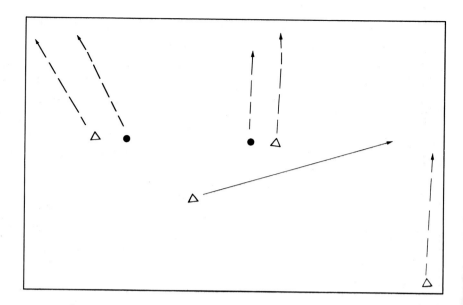

DIAGRAM X. THE BREAK-
REVERSE PASS. A runs to his
left before B passes the ball.

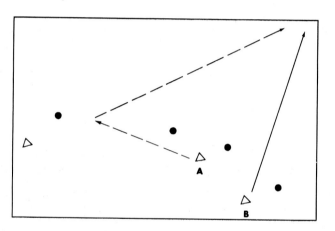

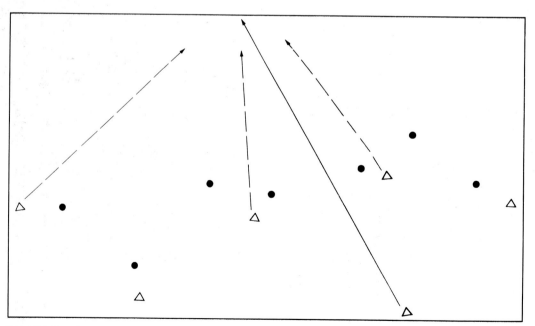

DIAGRAM Y. THE THROUGH PASS.

one way, then breaking his stride and reversing his direction to reach the open space into which the ball will be kicked.

The Through Pass

This is the most dangerous of all passes but is difficult to employ when the opposing defense has crowded its penalty area with reinforcements. It is best used when the opposing team has not regrouped after they have been attacking in your half. Diagram Y shows the obvious place for a through pass.

A word of warning: if either of the receiving attackers runs forward before the pass is kicked, he will be offside.

THE STRIKERS

No matter which of the team formations or passes are used, the offense must include strikers who can control the ball under great pressure, regardless of how it comes to them. Strikers must be able to take on the opposing defenders by dribbling and screening, and they must be adept at passing balls the first time to oncoming colleagues. They should be able to turn with the ball both to the left and right while confronted by tight-marking defenders, get up to the high ball to head it downwards into the goal, and above all learn how to take first-time shots whenever the slightest opening in the defense occurs.

The style of your offense will depend greatly upon the type of striker available to your team. If you have a tall striker who heads well, for example, high centers (crosses) from the wings would obviously be used more often than in a team comprised of short but speedy strikers. Conversely, the smaller striker will probably relish quick interpassing on the ground.

PHOTO 57. The NASL's Most Valuable Player of 1975 and the league's top scorer, Steve David of the Miami Toros shoots for goal. (Photo—John Pineda)

PHOTO 58. Jose Lopez of the Los Angeles Aztecs marks the illustrious and elusive Pele.

chapter **8**

DEFENSIVE SOCCER

Modern soccer, especially 4-3-3, requires that all players consider themselves defenders whenever their team loses the ball regardless of what position they play or what part of the field they are in. When possession is lost you and every member of your team must know what to do.

You will probably find it helpful if you think of defense as being divided into three separate sectors of the field: your own penalty area, midfield, and your opponent's penalty area. Although each sector has a different set of defensive problems and responsibilities, the aim in all three is the same: to regain possession of the ball. If possession is not possible, then containment is sought until other teammates can arrive to help out. And if efforts at possession and containment fail, then nearly everyone on your team retreats back into your own penalty area in order to seek numerical superiority.

DEFENDING IN YOUR OPPONENT'S PENALTY AREA

Once a striker loses the ball to his opponent's defense, he must try to regain possession by chasing and harassing the man with the ball. Even if possession is not achieved, the mere fact that his opponent is being challenged under pressure will quite often force him to pass hastily or make a mistake. It is always the striker nearest the opponent with the ball who chases him; the other strikers should be hurrying back toward their own half of the field, either covering advancing opponents or just simply getting back in case they are needed.

In addition to helping his own midfield-men and defenders by challenging his opponents in their own penalty area, there is always the chance that the striker will be able to steal the ball and start his own quick counterattack.

DEFENDING IN MIDFIELD

Unless there is a good possibility that you can get the ball away from your opponents, it is better not to tackle in midfield. Instead you should run with your opponent, staying goalside of him, and retreat back to your main line of defense. If you are playing a 4-3-3 formation you will most certainly have numerical superiority near and in your own penalty area, so it is there that you should commit yourself with vigorous tackling, not in midfield. If you tackle unsuccessfully and are left behind in midfield, it will be your opponents who will have numerical superiority—not you.

This concept of retreating defense (also called funneling) is very popular in mod-ern soccer, for it gives a defense the oppor-tunity to organize depth and to give each other close support. At the same time it permits the defenders to face their oppo-nents as they withdraw. This is an impor-tant consideration, since turning your back on an advancing opponent leaves you at a tremendous disadvantage and is one thing every experienced player tries to avoid whenever possible.

Another tactic used in midfield is called shepherding an opponent. In this situation the defender attempts to force the attacker to go in a certain direction, either by run-ning inside of him along the touchline (as in diagram Z) or by permitting him freedom and space so as to induce him to move toward other defenders (as in diagram AA).

Although the strategy behind shepherd-ing and retreating is to delay tackling until reaching your own defensive lines, you must, of course, step in and take posses-sion if your opponent should lose control of the ball as he is advancing.

DIAGRAM Z. SHEPHERDING AN OPPONENT AWAY FROM GOAL. A runs parallel with X, blocking his path toward goal and forcing him to run along the touchline until B, C, and D get back to help.

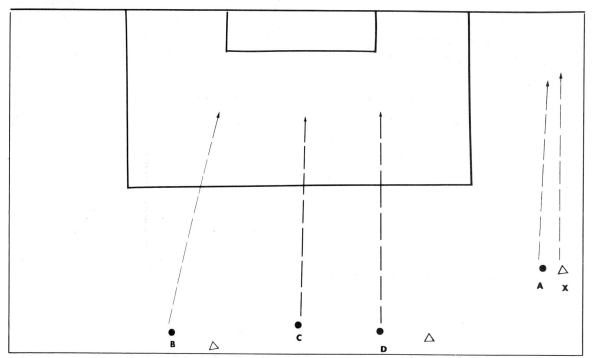

DIAGRAM AA. SHEPHERDING TOWARD OTHER DEFENDERS. A runs parallel to X, staying close to him but giving him ample room to move to his left.

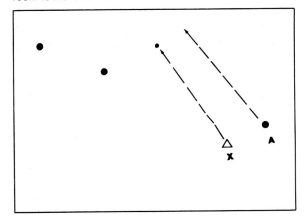

When defending in midfield it is very important that one of your strikers stays on the halfway line when everyone else is retreating back to your own penalty area. Not only will he insure that some defenders stay with him to guard him rather than joining in the attack against your own defense, but also he is in position to receive the long pass out from your own goalmouth to begin a counterattack.

DEFENDING IN YOUR OWN PENALTY AREA

Here is where the retreating has to come to an end. Now it's all close guarding of opponents, speedy covering of beaten teammates, and strong hard tackling. First of all, let's take a look at the two basic defensive systems used: man-to-man and zone defense.

Man-To-Man Defense

Just as in basketball, man-to-man means being assigned a specific opponent to cover, at least when he approaches your penalty area. Quite often it entails following your opponent no matter where he goes on the field, particularly if he is a key player for the opposition. Players like Pele and the brilliant Dutch star Johan Cruyff can expect to have one (and sometimes two) opponents shadowing them throughout a game.

The basic weakness of the man-to-man defense is that gaps result every time a defender is beaten. Because of this, most teams playing man-to-man use a "sweeper" as shown in diagram BB.

Another precautionary measure that some teams employing the man-to-man defense system rely upon is using the "free man" or "libero" in front of the defense. Usually a midfieldman, the free man challenges the opponent with the ball while the rest of the defenders stay with their assigned men. A strong free man out in front of the penalty area or a fast sweeper be-

DIAGRAM BB. MAN-TO-MAN DEFENSE WITH A SWEEPER.

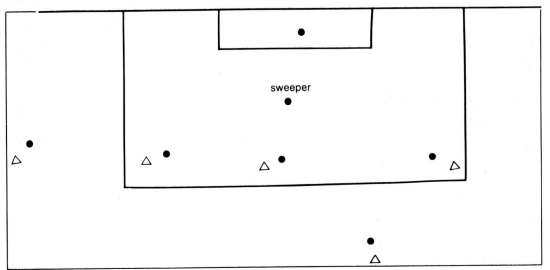

DIAGRAM CC. ZONE DEFENSE.   Shaded area shows responsibility of each defender.

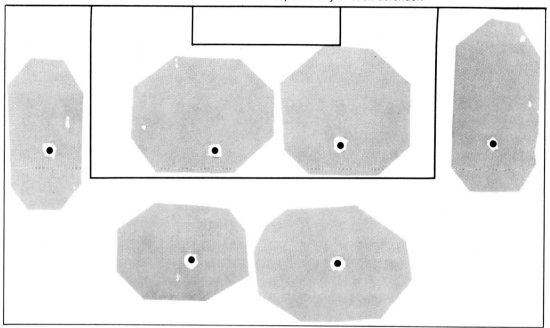

hind the defensive line can make a man-to-man defense hard to penetrate.

Zone Defense

Diagram CC shows at one glance the advantages and the disadvantage of the zone defense. By allowing each defender to patrol a specific area, the zone defense does not allow the defense to be pulled apart when opposing forwards begin to wander. There is also less chance of an overlap when each area is covered by a defender than there is in the man-to-man system, where quite often the attackers will all move to the right, for example, and thereby open up a nice gap for an overlap situation on the left.

The disadvantage of the zone, however, is the amount of space available to the attacking opponents. The remedy for this, as in the man-to-man system, is to use an extra man in defense (usually stationed in front of the defense in a midfield position).

Actually in recent years the trend has been to mix the man-to-man with the zone system. The weaknesses in both systems have been eliminated by employing the zone when the ball is in your opponent's half or until they approach your penalty area, and the man-to-man in and around the penalty area. Another variation is to play man-to-man against teams that do not interchange their positions and zone against teams that constantly have their forwards and midfieldmen switching.

Whatever system is used, the two center backs in modern soccer form the axis on which the rest of the defense turns. The center backs must move and turn with each change of direction of the opponents' attack, so that the back line forms a diagonal line. In this manner each defender is able to cover the teammate in front of him and to take his place if he is beaten. Diagram DD shows one of the two center backs ready to replace the beaten outside back. It is, of course, up to the outside back (in this case the left back) to run back into the defensive line and take the place of either the left center back (who has moved over to the advancing opponent), or to replace the right center back (who has moved over to take the left center back's place). This cycle of tackling, switching, tackling, and switching goes on indefinitely until the ball is either won or goes out of play.

PHOTO 59. Covering a teammate: Pat McBride (8) moves over to cover teammate Gary Rensing.

When defending in or around the penalty area, always place yourself goalside of your opponent (between him and your goal) and train yourself to be patient. As long as you bar the way his shot will be ineffective. The time to make your tackle is when he attempts to go past you. Never, never rush in blindly. If you get the opportunity to see the elegant Franz Becken-bauer of West Germany in action, note how unhurried he appears to be as he challenges his opponents. Beckenbauer, probably the calmest (and best) defender in the world, stays close to his opponent and waits for him to either make a mistake or push the ball too far ahead. He seems to know the exact time to make his tackle, and when he does he usually wins the ball.

DIAGRAM DD. DIAGONAL COVERING. Each defender stands ready to move across to cover for a teammate. If A is beaten, he runs back toward his own goal.

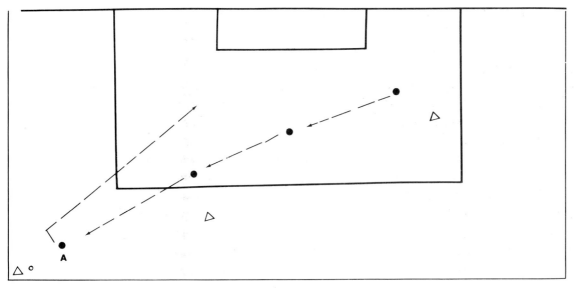

PHOTO 60. Archie Roboostoff of the San Jose Earthquakes and the U.S. national team practices his heading.

chapter 9
SELF-IMPROVEMENT EXERCISES

Although most soccer training is performed under the direction of the team coach, there are many skill exercises that the individual player should pursue on his own.

Soccer being essentially a running game, the first priority for any self-improvement campaign should be physical fitness, for there is no game that demands so much from its participants' physical reserves as soccer. Four, five, and sometimes six miles are run in a game, and unlike the long distance runner in a race, the soccer player is constantly breaking his stride to jog, walk, and sprint. It is a grueling stop-and-go style of running that cannot be duplicated by running three or four miles at a steady pace around a track. What is needed is a method that incorporates jogging, sprinting, and walking; such a method is interval running.

INTERVAL RUNNING

The purpose of interval running is to burden the body with intense stress alternated with recuperative periods of gentle stress. How far you should go, of course, depends upon your age and physical condition, but the ultimate aim is to increase the distance as often as possible until you can complete a two-mile session. Here's a suggested schedule for you to begin with:

1. Walk briskly for 25 yards, jog for 50 yards, then sprint for 25 yards. Repeat this sequence four times.

2. Do another sequence of the

above, but this time walk, jog, and sprint backwards.

3. Now go forward again, walking 10 yards, jogging 25 yards, and sprinting 50 yards. Repeat sequence twice.

4. Finally walk 10 yards, jog 50 yards, and sprint 25 yards. Repeat four times.

RUNNING WITH THE BALL AND DRIBBLING

Even though you may find it difficult at first to use your weaker foot, it is important to use alternate feet when practicing dribbling and running with the ball.

Get the feel of the ball by beginning your practice with a gentle tap-tap of the ball with the inside of the instep while jogging slowly. Place your weight on the balls of your feet and remember to turn your feet out. Gradually increase your speed to a faster jog and begin to turn in different directions, using the outside as well as the inside of the feet. Try stepping on the ball with the sole of the foot to stop it suddenly, then continue in the same direction.

Now speed up the pace and practice running with the ball. In the following exercises do not kick the ball too far ahead of you:

1. Jog with the ball for 25 yards, then sprint for another 25 yards, attempting to keep the ball directly in front of you. Don't forget: turn your toes inward, strike the ball as your foot touches the ground, and take short strides.

2. Repeat the above, but this time stop the ball dead with the sole of the foot at the end of the sprint.

3. Jog with the ball using the inside of the foot for the first 25 yards; then sprint 50 yards using the outside of the foot.

KICKING, TRAPPING, AND HEADING

When practicing kicking, trapping, and heading, let a wall act as your teammate. Of course, it is preferable to use a kick board if your team has one (kick boards are large wooden boards usually bigger than goal size), but for the following exercises, let's assume you will be using a wall.

Kicking

Most kicking on a soccer field is done while the ball is moving, so get into the habit of pushing the ball a few yards ahead of yourself before running onto it to kick. For a low instep kick, for instance, tap the ball with the outside of your right foot to the right of you, then as the ball is slowly rolling away take two or three steps to catch up with it with the right instep. Aim for a specific part of the wall (chalk up a target) and remember to keep the kicking knee over the ball. Repeat exercise using the left foot.

Practice the inside-of-the-foot kick and the outside-of-the-foot kick against the wall, again hitting the ball while it is moving.

Next, throw the ball against the wall. Let it bounce once or twice, then step into it with either foot and kick a volley. Repeat with a half volley. Try to keep the ball below chest height. To do this, you must lean over the ball.

Now try first-time kicking against the wall. The idea behind this exercise is to learn how to handle balls coming from different directions and at varying speeds. Kick softly at first; then as you proceed to kick with more power, move farther away from the wall. See how far back you can return the ball to the wall so that it comes right back to you. Use both feet and do not trap the ball.

Trapping

Stand 10 to 15 yards from the wall. Kick the ball at varying heights and speeds against the wall and trap the return ball, using the inside of the foot and then the sole of the foot.

Stand 20 to 25 yards away from the wall and kick low balls. Instead of trapping the ball dead, gently push at the ball as you trap it with the inside of the foot so that you can run with it up to the wall.

Now throw the ball and try cushioning the rebounds with the chest or thigh so that the ball drops immediately down to the feet.

Heading

Throw the ball against the wall. Get the forehead underneath the rebound and head it upwards. Then head the rebounds downwards, aiming for the bottom of the wall.

Use an underarm throw to make the ball rise from the wall a few inches higher than the head, and jump to reach the ball. Practice both the upward and downward headers.

Stand parallel to the wall. Throw the ball up above the head and jump up to meet it. Bend the upper trunk sideways and swing into the ball, turning the forehead toward the wall as it strikes the ball.

Now turn your back to the wall and practice heading backwards, jerking the head toward the wall upon contact.

Another good exercise for improving heading skills is to see how many times you can head the ball against the wall consecutively.

Juggling

No ball control practice would be complete without a little ball juggling; it's fun and it's a fine way to get the feel of the ball. It is also especially helpful when warming up for a game.

First practice getting the dead ball up into the air without resorting to using your hands. To do this, start with the ball a few feet in front of you. Place your weight on

PHOTO 61. Rod Johnson of the Chicago Sting warming up before a game with a little juggling. (Photo—Bill Smith)

PHOTO 62. The author's son, Mike Ruege, seen here training in Germany under the watchful eye of Germany's national junior goalie, Peter Sandhofe.

your nonkicking foot, then with your kicking foot step on the ball with the sole of the foot. Gently roll it back toward you; as you do so, take the same foot and place it under the ball so that the big toe, which is pointing upward, is able to flick the ball up into the air.

Once it is airborne let it fall onto the instep or the inside of the foot and proceed to tap it from one foot to the other. Try to keep the ball below knee height and keep the knees bent and flexible.

Let the ball go higher and use the middle of the thigh, chest, and forehead to hit the ball alternatively before it comes down again to the instep or the inside of the foot. See how long you can keep the ball in the air before it touches the ground. Twenty to thirty consecutive touches is what the beginner should strive for within his first year of soccer.

GOALKEEPER EXERCISES

I believe that a goalie should always have at least one other player with him at all practice sessions. However, with the wall as his helper, the goalie can at least practice the following simple exercises:

Stand 25 to 30 yards from the wall and practice the overarm, bowling, and javelin throws.

Stand about 10 yards from the wall and practice kicking with the instep kick. On the rebound try catching the ball. Do not dive unless there is grass or dirt available.

Stand about five yards from the wall and throw the ball underhand against the wall to make the ball rise above the head. Try saving the high rebound with either a two-handed catch, a two-handed punch, or a deflection.

Roll the ball against the wall so that it comes back to you on the ground. Bend down with the knees slightly bent for a two-handed pickup.

Finally, just because you're a goalkeeper doesn't mean you can skip the physical-fitness aspect of soccer. Indeed, it is essential that all goalkeepers be in top physical condition to withstand 90 minutes of soccer. Do your interval running and prepare yourself for the exhausting pressure training your coach undoubtedly has waiting for you.

PHOTO 63. Pele, the superstar of the North American Soccer League, avoids a slide tackle.

chapter 10
SOCCER IN AMERICA

The emergence of the United States as a full-fledged soccer-playing nation has been the most intriguing aspect of international soccer in the 1970s. All over the world immense interest in what is happening to soccer in the U.S. is clearly evident, and the general consensus is that now that the Americans are seriously involved in soccer it won't be long before they become a power to be reckoned with in the international arena.

The international family of soccer now numbers over 140 nations, all of whom (including the United States) are members of FIFA (Fédération Internationale de Football Association), headquartered in Zurich, Switzerland. All adult and junior players, both amateur and professional, come under FIFA's jurisdiction, and over 25 million players are registered.

Ever since it joined FIFA in 1913, the United States Soccer Association (formerly the United States Soccer Football Association) has struggled to put American soccer on an equal footing with soccer elsewhere. While foreign soccer organizations grew from little amateur clubhouses to multimillion-dollar operations with stadia holding up to 100,000 fans (over 200,000 spectators paid to see a game in Brazil in 1950), the American club's growth was minimal.

And yet at one time in the late 1800s it appeared that American soccer would be the sport of the masses. It was introduced to these shores by visiting British sailors and businessmen and the steady stream of British immigrants. The new British version of the age-old game of football (the Chinese played their *tsu chu* thousands of years ago) spread rapidly in the New England states and along the eastern seaboard. Between 1865 and 1875 it was the "in" sport among the prestigious Ivy League colleges and it had none of the "immigrant" sport connotation that it was later to acquire when millions of non-English-speaking peoples left Europe for America at the turn of the century.

In 1869 the famous Princeton vs. Rutgers contest, supposedly the first intercollegiate football game, was actually a soccer match. These two colleges, along with Harvard, Yale, and Columbia, were in the forefront of soccer's expansion.

But in 1874 Harvard played a game against McGill University of Canada using the rules of rugby football (a game derived from soccer and gradually gaining in popularity in Canadian college circles). Harvard liked what it saw and decided to switch to the hand-carrying game.

Harvard's decision to play all of its future "football" games according to rugby rules dealt American soccer a setback that would take 80 years to overcome, for within a few years the other colleges had followed Harvard's lead. The rugby rules were soon altered to produce a new game called "American football" (soccer is still called football in all countries but the U.S. and Canada). As the popularity of American football increased, interest in soccer declined until it was left to a handful of eastern prep schools, several small leagues, and, of course, the newly arriving immigrants to keep the game alive.

To their everlasting credit, the soccer pioneers of The United States Soccer Association, along with the high school and college associations, continued with their missionary work despite the apathy of most Americans. Over the years they gradually formed a nationwide network that was to prove so valuable when the soccer explosion of the last decade occurred.

The eighty years between 1875 and 1955

were decidedly bleak years for American soccer but were not without some auspicious moments. In 1904, for instance, the St. Rose team of St. Louis represented the United States in the final of the Olympic Games and was beaten 4-0 by Canada. In the same year the oldest soccer league still in existence in the United States, the Greater Los Angeles Soccer League, was formed, and in 1905 the first Intercollegiate Association was organized, with Columbia, Cornell, Harvard, Haverford, and Pennsylvania spearheading the drive to return soccer to the American colleges.

The twenties saw more amateur and semiprofessional leagues sprouting up everywhere, and soccer enjoyed a minor revival that was to last until the Depression. In 1922 the National Amateur Cup was offered for competition by the USSA. (The United States Challenge Cup begun in 1913 now became a competition for professionals only.) 1926 saw the birth of the Intercollegiate Soccer Football Association, which was soon followed by the formation of the National Soccer Coaches Association.

In 1930 the United States entered the first World Cup. Held every four years since, the World Cup is contested by all member nations belonging to FIFA and is now unquestionably the major international sports event, even overshadowing the Olympic Games. Most of FIFA's 140 nations participate in the preliminary qualifying rounds until only 16 teams remain to enter the finals. In 1930 the U.S. beat Belgium by a score of 3-0 in the first round of the finals. In the next round it defeated Paraguay by the same score, then lost to Argentina in the semifinal, 6-1. It was an outstanding achievement, notwithstanding the fact that most of the players were former British and European professionals.

In 1934, the U.S. again made it to the World Cup finals, but this time was unlucky enough to meet the eventual champion, Italy, in the first round and was eliminated by a score of 7-1.

Our greatest moment in international soccer was yet to come, for in 1950, the United States defeated the powerhouse of world soccer, England, in the opening round of the World Cup in Brazil. Although that team eventually eliminated itself, the United States victory over England is still considered the most sensational in international soccer history.

Since 1950 we have not been able to get to the finals, the main reason being the presence of the strong soccer nation Mexico in the preliminary qualifying rounds of the North American zone.

It was in the fifties that soccer finally began to expand among the American-born at both the high school and college levels. By 1959 over 250 high schools and over 100 colleges were fielding varsity teams. In the same year the first National Collegiate Soccer Tournament was held; not surprisingly, it was won by St. Louis University, the top college team of the past two decades. Its power base comes from the schools and junior clubs of St. Louis where for over 40 years soccer has flourished among the American-born even in the days when it was an "immigrant" sport elsewhere in the country. The highly organized structure of amateur soccer in St. Louis has produced more home-grown soccer stars than any other American city, and the St. Louis University's 10 National Collegiate championship teams since 1959 have been made up of nearly 100 percent local talent.

1966 saw the formation of two rival professional leagues, The United Soccer Association and the National Professional Soccer League. After huge financial losses, the two leagues merged into the North American Soccer League.

In 1969, the North American Soccer League (NASL), reduced from 17 to only five teams as an aftermath of the financial disaster, began to rebuild. The results have been startling: 20 cities now house NASL teams. The cost of getting a franchise in the NASL has risen from less than $100,000 in 1969 to $1,000,000 today.

The teams in the NASL are:

Boston Minutemen
Chicago Sting
Dallas Tornado
Hartford Bicentennials
Los Angeles Aztecs
Miami Toros
Minnesota Kicks
New York Cosmos
Philadelphia Atoms
Portland Timbers
Rochester Lancers
St. Louis Stars
San Antonio Thunder
San Diego Jaws
San Jose Earthquakes
Seattle Sounders
Tampa Bay Rowdies
Toronto Metros-Croatia
Vancouver Whitecaps
Washington Diplomats

Another pro league, smaller and less heavily financed than the NASL, is the American Soccer League (ASL), which was founded way back in the early thirties. Also rebounding from setbacks in the late sixties, the ASL has expanded from its traditional base on the Atlantic seaboard to cities across the nation, and now has 11 teams, including three teams in California.

The ASL teams are:

Chicago Cats
Cleveland Cobras
Connecticut Yankees
Golden Bay Buccaneers
Los Angeles Skyhawks
New Jersey Americans
New York Apollos
Rhode Island Oceaneers

PHOTO 64. Alex Skotarek of the
Chicago Sting.

Sacramento Spirits
Salt Lake City Golden Spikers
Tacoma Tide

With the increasing number of American schools and colleges turning to the sport (5,000 high schools and over 700 colleges), it was no surprise that the quality of soccer here improved greatly in the early seventies. In 1972, the young American Olympic soccer team fought its way through the Olympic qualifying rounds to win a place among the final 16 teams bound for Munich. Although eliminated very early in the tournament, losing two games and tying one, they impressed everyone with their potential.

Another significant indication that America was beginning to hold its own against foreign opposition came in 1973 when the powerful Polish national team, the 1972 Olympic champions, was beaten

1-0 by the full U.S. national team (pros as well as amateurs).

As for the future, it seems clear that American soccer will have an increasing impact on international soccer. The vastly improved coaching in our high schools and colleges is producing top-class material for our professional leagues to nurture into international stars. Young pros of the caliber of Bob Rigby (New York Cosmos), Mike Ivanow (San Jose Earthquakes), Dave D'Errico (Seattle Sounders), Bob Smith (New York Cosmos), Werner Roth (New York Cosmos), Chris Bahr (Philadelphia Atoms), Al Trost (St. Louis Stars), Joe Fink (Tampa Bay Rowdies), Archie Roboostoff (San Diego Jaws), Kyle Rote, Jr. (Dallas Tornado), Alex Skotarek (Chicago Sting), and Mani Hernandez (San Jose Earthquakes) form a pool of talent from which the U.S. can confidently choose a team that will provide a tough challenge to Mexico in the North American qualifying round of the 1978 World Cup.

What a great boost it would be for the American's "new sport" if Mexico were beaten and the United States team were to take that plane in June, 1978, for the World Cup final in Argentina!

appendix: laws of the game

The 1975 edition of the Laws of the Game is here reprinted with the kind permission of FIFA.

LAW I: THE FIELD OF PLAY

Dimensions

The field of play shall be rectangular, its length being not more than 130 yards nor less than 100 yards and its breadth not more than 100 yards and not less than 50 yards. (In International Matches the length shall be not more than 120 yards nor less than 110 yards and the breadth not more than 80 yards nor less than 70 yards.) The length shall in all cases exceed the breadth.

Marking

The field of play shall be marked with distinctive lines, not more than 5 inches in width, not by a V-shaped rut, in accordance with the plan, the longer boundary lines being called the touchlines and the shorter the goal lines. A flag on a post not less than 5 feet high, and having a non-pointed top, shall be placed at each corner; a similar flag post may be placed opposite the halfway line on each side of the field of play, not less than 1 yard outside the touchlines. A halfway line shall be marked out across the field of play. The center of the field of play shall be indicated by a suitable mark and a circle with a 10-yard radius shall be marked round it.

The Goal Area

At each end of the field of play two lines shall be drawn at right angles to the goal line, 6 yards from each goal post. These shall extend into the field of play for a distance of 6 yards and shall be joined by a line drawn parallel with the goal line. Each of the spaces enclosed by these lines and the goal line shall be called a goal area.

The Penalty Area

At each end of the field of play two lines shall be drawn at right angles to the goal line, 18 yards from each goal post. These shall extend into the field of play for a distance of 18 yards and shall be joined by a line drawn parallel with the goal line. Each of the spaces enclosed by these lines and the goal line shall be called a penalty area. A suitable mark shall be made within each penalty area, 12 yards from the midpoint of the goal line, measured along an undrawn line at right angles thereto. These shall be the penalty kick marks. From each penalty kick mark an arc of a circle, having a radius of 10 yards, shall be drawn outside the penalty area.

The Corner Area

From each corner flag post a quarter-circle, having a radius of 1 yard, shall be drawn inside the field of play.

The Goals

The goals shall be placed on the center of each goal line and shall consist of two upright posts, equidistant from the corner flags and 8 yards apart (inside measurement), joined by a horizontal crossbar the lower edge of which shall be 8 feet from the ground. The width and depth of the goal posts and the width and depth of the crossbars shall not exceed 5 inches (12 cm). The goal posts and the crossbars shall have the same width.

Nets may be attached to the posts, crossbars and ground behind the goals. They should be appropriately supported and be so placed as to allow the goalkeeper ample room.

Goal Nets

The use of nets made of hemp, jute or nylon is permitted. The nylon strings may, however, not be thinner than those made of hemp or jute.

LAW II: THE BALL

The ball shall be spherical; the outer casing shall be of leather or other approved materials. No material shall be used in its construction that might prove dangerous to the players.

The circumference of the ball shall not be more than 28 inches and not less than 27 inches. The weight of the ball at the start of the game shall not be more than 16 ounces nor less than 14 ounces. The pressure shall be equal to 0.6-0.7 atmosphere, which equals 9.0-10.5 lb/sq. in. (=600-700 gr/cm^2) at sea level. The ball shall not be changed during the game unless authorized by the Referee.

LAW III: NUMBER OF PLAYERS

(1) A match shall be played by two teams, each consisting of not more than eleven players, one of whom shall be the goalkeeper.

(2) Substitutes may be used in any match played under the rules of a competition, subject to the following conditions:

(a) that the authority of the international association(s) or national association(s) concerned has been obtained;

(b) that, subject to the restriction contained in the following paragraph (c), the rules of a competition shall state how many, if any, substitutes may be used; and

(c) that a team shall not be permitted to use more than two substitutes in any match.

(3) Substitutes may be used in any other match, provided that the two teams concerned reach agreement on a maximum number, not exceeding five, and that the terms of such agreement are disclosed to the Referee before the match. If the Referee is not informed, or the teams fail to reach agreement, no more than two substitutes shall be permitted.

(4) Any of the other players may change places with the goalkeeper, provided that the Referee is informed before the change is made, and provided also that the change is made during a stoppage in the game.

(5) When a goalkeeper or any other player is to be replaced by a substitute, the following conditions shall be observed:

(a) the Referee shall be informed of the proposed substitution before it is made;

(b) the substitute shall not enter the field of play until the player he is replacing has left, and then only after having received a signal from the Referee;

(c) he shall enter the field during a stoppage in the game, and at the halfway line.

Punishment

(a) Play shall not be stopped for an infringement of paragraph 4. The players concerned shall be cautioned immediately after the ball goes out of play.

(b) For any other infringement of this law, the player concerned shall be cautioned, and if the game is stopped by the Referee to administer the caution, it shall be restarted by an indirect free kick, to be taken by a player of the opposing team, from the place where the ball was when play was stopped.

LAW IV: PLAYERS' EQUIPMENT

(1) A player shall not wear anything that is dangerous to another player.

(2) Footwear (boots or shoes) must conform to the following standards:

(a) Bars shall be made of leather or rubber and shall be transverse and flat, not less than half an inch in width, and shall extend the total width of the sole and be rounded at the corners.

(b) Studs that are independently mounted on the sole and are replaceable shall be made of leather, rubber, aluminum, plastic or similar material and shall be solid. With the exception of that part of the stud forming the base, which shall not protrude from the sole more than one-quarter of an inch, studs shall be round in form and not less than half an inch in diameter. Where studs are tapered, the minimum diameter of any section of the stud must not be less than half an inch. Where metal seating for the screw type is used, this seating must be embedded in the sole of the footwear and any attachment screw shall be part of the stud. Other than the metal seating for the screw type of stud, no metal plates, even though covered with leather or rubber, shall be worn, nor studs that are threaded to allow them to be screwed on to a base screw that is fixed by nails or otherwise to the soles of footwear, nor studs that, apart from the base, have any form of protruding edge rim or relief marking or ornament.

(c) Studs that are molded as an integral part of the sole and are not replaceable shall be made of rubber, plastic, polyurethane or similar soft materials. Provided that there are no fewer than ten studs on the sole, they shall have a minimum diameter of $\frac{3}{8}$ inch (10mm). Additional supporting material to stabilize studs of soft materials, and ridges that do not protrude more than 5 mm from the sole and are molded to strengthen it, shall be permitted provided that they are in no way dangerous to other players. In all other respects they shall conform to the general requirements of this Law.

(d) Combined bars and studs may be worn, provided the whole conforms to the general requirements of this Law. Neither bars nor studs on the soles shall project more than $\frac{3}{4}$ inch. If nails are used, they shall be driven in flush with the surface.

(3) The goalkeeper shall wear colors that distinguish him from the other players and from the Referee.

Punishment

For any infringement of this Law, the player at fault shall be sent off the field of play to adjust his equipment and he shall not return without first reporting to the Referee, who shall satisfy himself that the player's equipment is in order; the player shall only reenter the game at a moment when the ball has ceased to be in play.

LAW V: REFEREES

A Referee shall be appointed to officiate in each game. His authority and the exercise of the powers granted to him by the Laws of the Game commence as soon as he enters the field of play.

His power of penalizing shall extend to offenses committed when play has been temporarily suspended, or when the ball is out of play. His decision on points of fact connected with the play shall be final, so far as the result of the game is concerned. He shall:

(a) Enforce the Laws.

(b) Refrain from penalizing in cases where he is satisfied that by doing so he would be giving an advantage to the offending team.

(c) Keep a record of the game; act as timekeeper and allow the full or agreed time, adding thereto all time lost through accident or other cause.

(d) Have discretionary power to stop the game for any infringement of the Laws and to suspend or terminate the game whenever, by reason of the elements, interference by spectators or other cause, he deems such stoppage necessary. In such a case he shall submit a detailed report to the competent authority, within the stipulated time, and in accordance with the provisions set up by the National Association under whose jurisdiction the match was played. Reports will be deemed to be made when received in the ordinary course of postal service.

(e) From the time he enters the field of play, caution any player guilty of misconduct or ungentlemanly behavior, and if he persists, suspend him from further participation in the game. In such cases the Referee shall send the name of the offender to the competent authority, within the stipulated time, and in accordance with the provisions set up by the National Association under whose jurisdiction the match was played. Reports will be deemed to be made when received in the ordinary course of postal service.

(f) Allow no person other than the players and the linesmen to enter the field of play without his permission.

(g) Stop the game if, in his opinion, a player has been seriously injured; have the player removed as soon as possible from the field of play, and immediately resume the game. If a player is slightly injured, the game shall not be stopped until the ball has ceased to be in play. A player who is able to go to the touchline or goal line for attention of any kind shall not be treated on the field of play.

(h) Send off the field of play any player who, in his opinion, is guilty of violent conduct, serious foul play or the use of foul or abusive language.

(i) Signal for recommencement of the game after all stoppages.

(j) Decide that the ball provided for a match meets with the requirements of Law II.

LAW VI: LINESMEN

Two linesmen shall be appointed, whose duty (subject to the decision of the Referee) shall be to indicate when the ball is out of play and which side is entitled to the corner kick, goal kick or throw-in. They shall also assist the Referee to control the game in accordance with the Laws. In the event of undue interference or improper conduct by a linesman, the Referee shall dispense with his services and arrange for a substitute to be appointed. (The matter shall be reported by the Referee to the competent authority.) The linesmen should be equipped with flags by the club on whose ground the match is played.

LAW VII: DURATION OF THE GAME

The duration of the game shall be two equal periods of 45 minutes, unless otherwise mutually agreed upon, subject to the following:

(a) Allowance shall be made in either period for all time lost through accident or other cause, the amount of which shall be a matter for the discretion of the Referee;

(b) Time shall be extended to permit a penalty kick being taken at or after the expiration of the normal period in either half.

At halftime the interval shall not exceed 5 minutes, except by consent of the Referee.

LAW VIII: THE START OF PLAY

(a) At the beginning of the game, choice of ends and the kickoff shall be decided by the toss of a coin. The team winning the toss shall have the option of choice of ends or the kickoff. The Referee having given a signal, the game shall be started by a player taking a place kick (i.e., a kick at the ball while it is stationary on the ground in the center of the field of play) into his opponents' half of the field of play. Every player shall be in his own half of the field and every player of the team opposing that of the kicker shall remain not less than 10 yards from the ball until it is kicked off; it shall not be deemed in play until it has traveled the distance of its own circumference. The kicker shall not play the ball a second time until it has been touched or played by another player.

(b) After a goal has scored, the game shall be restarted in like manner by a player of the team losing the goal.

(c) After halftime, when restarting the game, ends shall be changed and the kickoff shall be taken by a player of the opposite team to that of the player who started the game.

Punishment

For any infringement of this Law, the kickoff shall be retaken, except in the case of the kicker playing the ball again before it has been touched or played by another player; for this offense, an indirect free kick shall be taken by a player of the opposing team from the place where the infringement occurred. A goal shall not be scored direct from a kickoff.

(d) After any other temporary suspension of play for any cause not mentioned elsewhere in these Laws, provided that immediately prior to the suspension the ball has not passed over the touchline or goal line, when restarting the game, the Referee shall drop the ball at the place where it was when play was suspended and it shall be deemed in play when it has touched the ground; if, however, it goes over the touchline or goal line after it has been dropped by the Referee but before it is touched by a player, the Referee shall again drop it. A player shall not play the ball until it has touched the ground. If this section of the Law is not complied with, the Referee shall again drop the ball.

LAW IX: BALL IN AND OUT OF PLAY

The ball is out of play:

(a) When it has wholly crossed the goal line or touchline, whether on the ground or in the air.

(b) When the game has been stopped by the Referee.

The ball is in play at all other times from the start of the match to the finish including:

(a) If it rebounds from a goal post, crossbar or corner flag post into the field of play.

(b) If it rebounds off either the Referee or linesmen when they are in the field of play.

(c) In the event of a supposed infringement of the Laws, until a decision is given.

LAW X: METHOD OF SCORING

Except as otherwise provided by these Laws, a goal is scored when the whole of the ball has passed over the goal line, between the goal posts and under the crossbar, provided it has not been thrown, carried or intentionally propelled by hand or arm by a player of the attacking side, except in the case of a goalkeeper, who is within his own penalty area.

The team scoring the greater number of goals during a game shall be the winner; if no goals or an equal number of goals are scored, the game shall be termed a "draw."

LAW XI: OFFSIDE

A player is offside if he is nearer his opponent's goal line than the ball *at the moment the ball is played unless:*

(a) He is in his own half of the field of play.

(b) There are two of his opponents nearer to their own goal line than he is.

(c) The ball last touched an opponent or was last played by him.

(d) He receives the ball direct from a goal kick, a corner kick, a throw-in, or when it was dropped by the Referee.

Punishment

For an infringement of this Law, an indirect free kick shall be taken by a player of the opposing team from the place where the infringement occurred.

A player in an offside position shall not be penalized unless, in the opinion of the Referee, he is interfering with the play or with an opponent, or is seeking to gain an advantage by being in an offside position.

LAW XII: FOULS AND MISCONDUCT

A player who intentionally commits any of the following nine offenses:

(a) Kicks or attempts to kick an opponent;

(b) Trips an opponent, i.e., throws or attempts to throw him by the use of the legs or by stooping in front of or behind him;

(c) Jumps at an opponent;

(d) Charges an opponent in a violent or dangerous manner;

(e) Charges an opponent from behind unless the latter is obstructing;

(f) Strikes or attempts to strike an opponent;

(g) Holds an opponent;

(h) Pushes an opponent;

(i) Handles the ball, i.e., carries, strikes or propels the ball with his hand or arm. (This does not apply to the goalkeeper within his own penalty area);

shall be penalized by the award of a direct free kick to be taken by the opposing side from the place where the offense occurred.

Should a player of the defending side intentionally commit one of the above nine offenses within the penalty area he shall be penalized by a *penalty kick.*

A penalty kick can be awarded irrespective of the position of the ball, if in play, at the time an offense within the penalty area is committed.

A player committing any of the five following offenses:

1. Playing in a manner considered by the Referee to be dangerous, e.g., attempting to kick a ball held in the hands of a goalkeeper;

2. Charging fairly, i.e., with the shoulder, when the ball is not within playing distance of the players concerned and they are definitely not trying to play it;

3. When not playing the ball, intentionally obstructing an opponent, i.e., running between the opponent and the ball, or interposing the body so as to form an obstacle to an opponent;

4. Charging the goalkeeper except when he

(a) is holding the ball;

(b) is obstructing an opponent;

(c) has passed outside his goal area;

5. When playing as a goalkeeper,

(a) takes more than four steps while holding, bouncing or throwing the ball in the air and catching it again without releasing it so that it is played by another player; or

(b) indulges in tactics which, in the opinion of the Referee, are designed merely to hold up the game and thus waste time and so give an unfair advantage to his own team

shall be penalized by the award of an *indirect free kick* to be taken by the opposing side from the place where the infringement occurred.

A player shall be *cautioned* if:

(j) he enters or reenters the field of play to join or rejoin his team after the game has commenced, or leaves the field of play during the progress of the game (except through accident) without, in either case, first having received a signal from the Referee showing that he may do so. If the Referee stops the game to administer the caution, the game shall be restarted by an indirect free kick taken by a player of the opposing team from the place where the ball was when the Referee stopped the game. If, however, the offending player has committed a more serious offense he shall be penalized according to that section of the Law he infringed;

(k) he persistently infringes the Laws of the Game;

(l) he shows by word or action, dissent from any decision given by the Referee;

(m) he is guilty of ungentlemanly conduct.

For any of the last three offenses, in addition to the caution, an *indirect free kick* shall also be awarded to the opposing side from the place where the offense occurred unless a more serious infringement of the Laws of the Game was committed.

A player shall be *sent off* the field of play if:

(n) in the opinion of the Referee he is guilty of violent conduct or serious foul play;

(o) he uses foul or abusive language;

(p) he persists in misconduct after having received a caution.

If play be stopped by reason of a player being ordered from the field for an offense without a separate breach of the Law having been committed, the game shall be resumed by an *indirect free kick* awarded to the opposing side from the place where the infringement occurred.

LAW XIII: FREE KICK

Free kicks shall be classified under two headings: "Direct" (from which a goal can be scored direct against the offending side), and "Indirect" (from which a goal cannot be scored unless the ball has been played or touched by a player other than the kicker before passing through the goal).

When a player is taking a direct or an indirect free kick inside his own penalty area, all of the opposing players shall remain outside the area, and shall be at least 10 yards from the ball while the kick is being taken. The ball shall be in play immediately after it has traveled the distance of its own circumference and is beyond the penalty area. The goalkeeper shall not receive the ball into his hands, in order that he may thereafter kick it into play. If the ball is not kicked direct into play, beyond the penalty area, the kick shall be retaken. When a player is taking a direct or an indirect free kick outside his own penalty area, all of the opposing players shall be at least 10 yards from the ball until it is in play, unless they are standing on their own goal line between the goal posts. The ball shall be in play when it has traveled the distance of its own circumference.

If a player of the opposing side encroaches into the penalty area, or within 10 yards of the ball, as the case may be, before a free kick is taken, the Referee shall delay the taking of the kick, until the Law is complied with.

The ball must be stationary when a free kick is taken and the kicker shall not play the ball a second time, until it has been touched or played by another player.

Punishment

If the kicker, after taking the free kick, plays the ball a second time before it has been touched or played by another player, an indirect free kick shall be taken by a player of the opposing team from the spot where the infringement occurred.

LAW XIV: PENALTY KICK

A penalty kick shall be taken from the penalty mark, and when it is being taken, all players, with the exception of the player taking the kick and the opposing goalkeeper, shall be within the field of play but outside the penalty area, and at least 10 yards from the penalty mark. The opposing goalkeeper must stand (without moving his feet) on his own goal line, between the goalposts, until the ball is kicked. The player taking the kick must kick the ball forward; he shall not play the ball a second time until it has been touched or played by another player. The ball shall be deemed in play directly after it is kicked, i.e., when it has traveled the distance of its circumference, and a goal may be scored direct from such a penalty kick. If the ball touches the goalkeeper before passing between the posts when a penalty kick is being taken at or after the expiration of halftime or fulltime, it does not nullify a goal. If necessary, time of play shall be extended at halftime or fulltime to allow a penalty kick to be taken.

Punishment

For any infringement of this Law:

(a) by the defending team, the kick shall be retaken if a goal has not resulted.

(b) by the attacking team, other than by the player taking the kick, if a goal is scored it shall be disallowed and the kick retaken.

(c) by the player taking the penalty kick, committed after the ball is in play, a player of the opposing team shall take an indirect free kick from the spot where the infringement occurred.

LAW XV: THROW-IN

When the whole of the ball passes over a touchline, either on the ground or in the air, it shall be thrown in from the point where it crossed the line, in any direction, by a player of the team opposite that of the player who last touched it. The thrower at the moment of delivering the ball must face the field of play and part of each foot shall be either on the touchline or on the ground outside the touchline. The thrower shall use both hands and shall deliver the ball from behind and over his head. The ball shall be in play immediately after it enters the field of play, but the thrower shall not again play the ball until it has been touched or played by another player. A goal shall not be scored direct from a throw-in.

Punishment

(a) If the ball is improperly thrown in, the throw-in shall be taken by a player of the opposing team.

(b) If the thrower plays the ball a second time before it has been touched or played by another player, an indirect free kick shall be taken by a player of the opposing team from the place where the infringement occurred.

LAW XVI: GOAL KICK

When the whole of the ball passes over the goal line, excluding that portion between the goal posts, either in the air or on the ground, having last been played by one of the attacking team, it shall be kicked direct into play beyond the penalty area from a point within that half of the goal area nearest to where it crossed the line by a player of the defending team. A goalkeeper shall not receive the ball into his hands from a goal kick in order that he may thereafter kick it into play. If the ball is not kicked beyond the penalty area, i.e., direct into play, the kick shall be retaken. The kicker shall not play the ball a second time until it has touched—or been played by—another player. A goal shall not be scored direct from such a kick. Players of the team opposing that of the player taking the goal kick shall remain outside the penalty area while the kick is being taken.

Punishment

If a player taking a goal kick plays the ball a second time after it has passed beyond the penalty area, but before it has been touched or been played by another player, an indirect free kick shall be awarded to the opposing team, to be taken from the place where the infringement occurred.

LAW XVII: CORNER KICK

When the whole of the ball passes over the goal line, excluding that portion between the goal posts, either in the air or on the ground, having last been played by one of the defending team, a member of the attacking team shall take a corner kick, i.e., the whole of the ball shall be placed within the quarter-circle at the nearest corner flag-post, which must not be moved, and it shall be kicked from that position. A goal may be scored direct from such a kick. Players of the team opposing that of the player taking the corner kick shall not approach within 10 yards of the ball until it is in play, i.e., it has traveled the distance of its own circumference, nor shall the kicker play the ball a second time until it has been touched or played by another player.

Punishment

(a) If the player who takes the kick plays the ball a second time before it has been touched or played by another player, the Referee shall award an indirect free kick to the opposing team, to be taken from the place where the infringement occurred.

(b) For any other infringement the kick shall be retaken.

Backs: The defenders: right back, right center back, left center back, and left back.

Caution: A warning by the referee to a player who persistently fouls, who argues with the referee, or who is guilty of bad sportsmanship.

Center: To kick the ball from the wing into the center of the field, usually into the opponent's penalty area. Also described as crossing the ball.

Center back: A defender positioned in the center of the defensive line.

Center circle: A circle with a ten-yard radius in the middle of the field.

Center forward: See striker.

Charge: Use of the shoulder to attempt to knock an opponent off balance. It is the only legal charge in soccer.

Chip pass: A pass that rises quickly.

Clearance: A kick or header by a defender, or a kick or throw by a goalkeeper that moves the ball out of the penalty area. Generally the clearance is made during moments of extreme pressure.

Corner area: Marked by a small arc, the corner area is located at the four corners of the field and is the place from which corner kicks are taken.

Corner kick: Also called a corner, the corner kick is a direct free kick from which a goal can be scored directly. It is taken at the corner arc and is awarded to the offensive team when a member of the defensive team last touches the ball before it passes over the goal line. You cannot be offside directly from a corner kick.

Cover: A. Guarding an opponent (see Marking). **B.** Supporting a teammate by being prepared to take over from him if he is beaten by an opponent.

Cross: See Center.

Dangerous play: Any action by a player that the referee considers to be dangerous or likely to cause injury. The two most common examples are kicking a shoulder-high ball when an opponent is attempting to head the ball, and lowering the head to head a ball lower than the chest when an opponent is trying to kick it.

Dead ball: Whenever the ball is not in play it is considered dead. This includes every time the ball goes over the goal lines or touchlines and whenever the referee whistles for an infraction or stops play.

Direct free kick: Awarded for the most serious infractions. The kick is taken from the place the foul occurred; a goal can be scored directly from the kick.

Dribbling: Using the feet to move the ball through or around opponents. Usually consists of a series of short taps and pushes.

Drop ball: Used to restart the game after the referee has stopped play for some reason other than an infringement of the laws. The referee drops the ball between two opposing players. It is not in play until it touches the ground, and if a player touches it beforehand then it must be dropped again.

Far post: The goal post farthest from the man who has the ball. Your coach will probably ask you to aim for the "near post" or "far post" especially when you are centering the ball from the wings.

Feint: A movement of the shoulder, hips, legs, and other parts of the body to deceive or confuse an opponent.

First-time: Kicking or heading the ball as it comes to you without attempting to control it. Also referred to as one-touch.

Forward: Offensive player.

Foul: An infraction of the Laws of the Game.

Free kick: A kick awarded when an infraction has been committed. Taken from the spot where the infraction occurred, the free kick can either be direct or indirect. All opponents must be ten yards away from the ball when the kick is taken.

Give-and-go: See Wall pass.

Goal area: The twenty-by-six-yard box in front of the goal.

Goal kick: Awarded to the defending team whenever an opponent is the last to touch the ball before it crosses over the goal line. The kick must be taken from inside the goal area.

Goal line: The boundary line that runs along the width of the field.

Goal nets: Nets attached to the goalposts and the ground.

Half volley: A ball kicked just as it is rebounding off the ground.

Halfway line: The line that runs from touchline to touchline across the midway point of the field and which divides the field into two equal halves.

Hands: The general term used when the ball is touched with the hands or arms by a player other than a goalkeeper.

Heading: A method of propelling the ball by means of the head (usually the forehead).

Holding: To obstruct an opponent's progress or movement by the use of your hands.

Indirect free kick: A kick given for minor infractions of the laws in which the kicker cannot score directly.

Inswinger: A corner kick that curves into the goal.

Interception: Getting to the ball to cut it off before it reaches its intended receiver.

Kickoff: A kick from the center spot which starts the game at the beginning of each period and after each goal is scored.

Lateral pass: A pass that goes across the field.

Linesmen: The two officials who assist the referee, mainly to indicate which team should be awarded throw-ins and when a player is offside.

Linkman: See midfieldman.

Man-to-man defense: Each member of the defense is given a specific opponent to guard (or mark).

Marking: Shadowing or guarding an opponent.

Midfieldman: Formerly called a halfback, the midfieldman supports both his defensive and offensive teammates and is the link between both groups.

Obstruction: An attempt to impede or prevent an opponent from moving with or without the ball by blocking his path.

Offside: A player who is nearer to his opponent's goal line than the ball when the ball is played to him is offside unless:

1. There are two opponents nearer to the goal line.
2. He is in his own half of the field.
3. The ball last touches an opponent.
4. He receives the ball directly from a corner kick, goal kick, throw-in, or a drop ball.

Off the ball: Running without the ball to seek space or to support a teammate with the ball.

Outside left: The left winger or left outside striker.

Outside right: The right winger or right outside striker.

Outswinger: A corner kick that curves out away from the goal.

Overlapping: A player, usually a defender, running ahead of his winger along the touchline into an unguarded area.

Own goal: A goal accidentally scored by a player against his own team. In soccer he gets the credit for the goal even if it is only a deflection of an opponent's shot.

Pass: The movement of the ball from one teammate to another.

Penalty area: The 44-by-18-yard box in front of the goal.

Penalty kick: Any direct free kick awarded to the offensive team in the penalty area. The kick is taken from the penalty spot and only the kicker and the goalkeeper can remain in the penalty area while it is being taken.

Penalty shot: Twelve yards from the goal.

Pitch: An English term for the field but quite often used in the U.S.

Punt: A kick used by goalkeepers when attempting long clearances. The ball is dropped by the hands and kicked before it reaches the ground.

Save: Any catch or deflection made by the goalkeeper.

Screening: Keeping your body between your opponent and the ball.

Shepherding: Attempting to force your opponent in a desired direction while retreating back toward your own goal.

Shot: A kick at your opponent's goal with the intention of scoring.

Shoulder charge: See Charge.

Striker: The player positioned in the center of the offensive line, formerly known as center forward.

Sweeper: A defender who plays behind the defensive line to counter any breakthrough.

Switch: An exchange of positions by two or more players in order to support each other or to confuse opponents.

Tackling: An attempt to dispossess an opponent of the ball by use of the feet.

Throw-in: A restart consisting of a two-handed throw over the head whenever the ball crosses over the touchline.

Touchlines (sidelines): The boundary lines drawn along the outside lengths of the field.

Trapping: Killing the ball with some part of the body other than the hands and arms.

Volley: A ball kicked while it is in the air.

Wall Pass: A pass to a teammate who returns it to you first-time so that you can run past an intervening opponent and collect the ball in an unguarded space. Your teammate actually acts in the manner of a wall.

Wing: The area of the field along the touchlines.

Winger: The outside strikers, also called outside right and outside left.

Zone defense: Each member of the defense is given a specific area to guard.

index